MONOGRAPH SERIES IN WORLD AFFAIRS

VOLUME FIFTEEN

UNIVERSITY OF DENVER

Graduate School of International Studies

VOLUME FIFTEEN

Book One
ARABESQUE: UNTANGLING THE PATTERNS OF
CONVENTIONAL ARMS SUPPLY TO ISRAEL AND THE ARAB STATES
AND THE IMPLICATIONS FOR UNITED STATES POLICY
ON SUPPLY OF "LETHAL" WEAPONS TO EGYPT
Lewis W. Snider

•

Book Two
THE SEABED ARMS CONTROL NEGOTIATIONS:
A STUDY OF MULTILATERAL ARMS CONTROL DIPLOMACY
Bennett Ramberg

•

Book Three
THE POLITICAL ECONOMY OF PUBLIC GOODS
AND INTERNATIONAL COOPERATION
Todd Sandler, William J. Loehr, Jon T. Cauley

•

Book Four
ETHNO-NATIONALISM, MULTINATIONAL CORPORATIONS,
AND THE MODERN STATE
Ronald Grant, E. Spencer Wellhofer, Editors

ETHNO-NATIONALISM, MULTINATIONAL CORPORATIONS, AND THE MODERN STATE

Ronald M. Grant, E. Spencer Wellhofer
Editors

MONOGRAPH SERIES IN WORLD AFFAIRS

Volume Fifteen
Book Four

Ethno-nationalism, multinational corporations, and the modern state.

(Monograph series in world affairs; v. 15, book 4)
Includes bibliographical references.
1. International business enterprises—Social aspects—Addresses, essays, lectures. 2. Nationalism—Addresses, essays, lectures. 3. National state—Addresses, essays, lectures. I. Enloe, Cynthia H., 1938-   II. Grant, Ronald M. III. Wellhofer, E. Spencer, 1941-   IV. Series: Denver. University. Social Science Foundation. Monograph series in world affairs; v. 15, book 4.
HD2755.5.E86   338.8'8   78-74237

ISBN 0-87940-057-9
ISSN 0077-0582

ABOUT THE AUTHORS

RONALD M. GRANT is Assistant Professor of Political Science at the University of Denver. A specialist in Indonesian politics, he was a Fulbright fellow to that country in 1973, and served as a program development consultant in Indonesia through AID in 1977. He has presented numerous papers on Indonesian administration and administrative politics. His most recent publication appears in *Asian Survey,* entitled "Indonesia: 1978."

E. SPENCER WELLHOFER is Assistant Professor of Political Science at the University of Denver. He has published in several academic journals in the fields of comparative politics and political sociology. His current interests are in longitudinal process models of change.

CYNTHIA H. ENLOE is Professor of Government at Clark University and serves as chairman of the Social Science Research Council's Committee on Ethnicity. Among her published works are *Ethnic Conflict and Political Development* (1973), *Police, Military and Ethnicity: Foundations of State Power* (forthcoming, 1979), and *Ethnic Soldiers: State Security in Divided Societies* (forthcoming, 1979).

PHILLIP RAWKINS teaches politics at Ryerson Polytechnical Institute in Toronto, where he is also coordinator of the Third World Centre. He completed his Ph.D. in 1975 with a dissertation on Welsh nationalism. Presently his work focuses on nationalism, ethnicity, and the education of minority-language groups.

PIERRE-MICHEL FONTAINE is an Associate Professor of Political Science at UCLA and a faculty Research Associate at UCLA's Center for Afro-American Studies. He has published several articles on Latin America and the Caribbean. A forthcoming book is entitled *The United Nations and the Problems of Dependency and Underdevelopment in Latin America: The Experience of Ecla.*

LESLIE I. HILL serves as the Director of Research and Program Development at the Atlanta Black United Fund and holds positions with the City of Atlanta Community Relations Commission and the Atlanta Commission on the Status of Women. She holds a bachelor's degree from Barnard College, and is a Ph.D. candidate at Atlanta University. Recent publications include: "History of Black Struggle in America: 1966-1972" (forthcoming) and "A History of Afro-American Music," printed by the Atlanta University School of Social Work.

PAUL SHANKMAN teaches anthropology at the University of Colorado, Boulder. He has done field research in Western Samoa and has written about problems of underdevelopment in Oceania. Among his publications are articles on multinational timbering operations in Western Samoa reported in *Natural History Magazine,* October 1975, and a monograph on migration, *Migration and Underdevelopment: The Case of Western Somoa,* Westview Press, 1976.

TABLE OF CONTENTS

INTRODUCTION

Ronald M. Grant and E. Spencer Wellhofer

On first consideration, ethno-nationalism, multinational corporations, and the modern state would not appear subject to simultaneous investigation. Each suggests a different level of social organization, a distinct legitimacy, and variation in goals. Ethnic identity and ethno-nationalism are phenomena associated in the past with "transitional" societies; overcoming ethnic identification was part of "nation building." Multinational corporations are outgrowths of highly industrialized states, crossing geography and sovereignty in the pursuit of economic profit. Ethno-nationalism forms upon affective attachment, while the multinational corporation exemplifies technology, capital, and bureaucratic rationale.

The essays in this monograph deal with these phenomena separately, and examine the relationships between them at three levels: internally, whole-society, and cross-nationally. Ethno-nationalism is a movement identified with a minority of a larger society, even when cross-cutting state boundaries. The movement's legitimacy draws upon affective, reactive, and collective orientations. The modern state is an organization defined by legal boundaries, draws legitimacy from affective and collective goods, and is based upon legal-rational authority. Multinational corporations pursue material resources and profits in the marketplace and emphasize technological rationality. Such organizations transcend state and ethnic boundaries, and operate on a strict political economy calculus. Noneconomic interests and goals are secondary.

Originating from a conference at the University of Denver in June 1976 titled "Challenges to the Nation State: Ethnicity and the Emerging Economic World Order," these papers, in addressing the main topic, give support to an increasingly popular perception about ethnic identity and its role in the contemporary world. Specifically, the positions advanced by several authors indicate ethnic identity is not fading away, but rather is persisting and even reemerging in modern industrial states as well as in developing societies.[1] The persistence of ethno-nationalism as a major element in understanding modern state politics is stimulated by economic issues including those of production control, employment opportunities, income and wage distribution, where policy is frequently set by economic groups geographically far removed from those groups expressing discontent. In the past, ethnic conflict over economic issues most often pivoted on a center-periphery cleavage within a specific society or state.[2] With the development of international economic interdependence, a new dimension emerged: the center-periphery struggle acquired international aspects.

1

The internationalization of the center-periphery cleavages captures some aspects of the division between First and Third Worlds, but does not encompass the thrust of this monograph. Our emphasis remains with the internal dynamics of specific societies.

Over past decades MNCs and other types of multinational organizations—the European Economic Community, the Organization of Petroleum Exporting Countries—have stimulated ethnic awareness through ethnic discrimination practices. Multinational economic organizations disrupt traditional economic markets dominated by ethnic or regional groups. In addition, they strengthen the state and those who control it *vis-à-vis* ethnic minorities.

Minority and ethnic movements then pose a challenge to the state not simply in terms of the elusive concept of sovereignty, but tangibly in the area of social and economic stability. New international economic organizations mobilize forces potentially disruptive to the status quo. Since this process is poorly understood, the Denver conference focused on the relationship between the internationalization of the economy and the growth of ethno-nationalism.

MNCs and other multinational economic alliances initially offer tantalizing benefits to the state. Later, however, MNCs may exasperate ethnic tensions by discriminatory policies, inequitable exchanges, and reinforcement of the status quo. Minority and ethno-nationalist movements are one major reaction to injustices, and ethno-nationalism serves to legitimize a challenge to the ruling elite and to the social order.

During the conference we examined the relationship between ethnicity and multinational economic organizations, and explored the linkages between these across the three levels of political organization: sub-national, national, and cross-national.[3] Accordingly, the conference was subdivided into three panels. The first dealt with ethnicity as a potential problem for the state.[4] The second focused on the MNCs' effect on various groups, regardless of ethnicity and ethno-nationalism, and the resulting challenge to the state, specifically in terms of class conflict. The third dealt with the effect of multinational economic organizations on ethnic divisions and cleavages within societies, with ethno-nationalism as a response to these forces, and with the resulting challenge to the state and to the prevailing social order.

Professor Enloe's paper provides an overview of the MNC in the developing world. She points out several parallels between the MNC and its forerunner, the colonial-era trading company. Her opening statement, that modern companies "have always shaped ethnic identities and inter-ethnic distributions of power," sets the tone. Enloe analyzes linkages across levels of political organization. Not only does she consider the MNC's impact on ethnic identifications, but also she draws together a wide array of examples illustrating responses of ethnic groups to the multinational corporation.

Professor Shankman discusses the development of economic inequalities resulting from rapid growth produced by an alliance of the MNC and the host government through the case study method. In the context of Brazil he vividly illustrates the economic dislocations which result from an infusion of foreign capital, technology, and external resources brought about with the arrival of the MNC. Unplanned and rapid internal migrations, crowding of already overpopulated cities, excessive burdens on public services, disruption of local cottage and small-scale industries, and the conspicuous spending of elites are frequently noted consequences of a rapid inflow of foreign capital and technology. Shankman demonstrates that Brazil is no exception to the pattern.

Shankman's essay is important in this collection because it provides evidence for an unexpected consequence: the debilitating effect of the MNC produced no increase of ethnic identification in Brazil. Rather, its effects are to be interpreted in terms of social class identity. The emergence of ethnic identities and ethno-nationalism cannot be separated from the class composition of the society. The case of Brazil is striking. Though Brazil is an ethnically and regionally diverse society of a hundred million people, no important minority nationalism presented a significant challenge to the MNC or to its alliance with the present government.

Over the last several years, Brazil has pursued a more "liberal" policy toward the expression of discontent with the society. There has since been criticism of the role of the MNC and even governmental skepticism toward its overall impact on the society. Yet the lack of any ethno-national response to the state multinational economic alliance makes Brazil's an intriguing case. It highlights the fact that general models to explain the emergence of ethno-nationalism cannot be based on single factors. Brazil's social evolution has not provided the essential cultural distinctions critical for attachments beyond class stratification. Its recent economic upsurge resulted in a cooptation and/or elimination of the rural *petite bourgeoisie,* the principal class sector capable of supplying the necessary materials and intellectual resources for a minority nationalistic challenge.

The study of Brazil serves as a counterfoil to the other papers, which explicitly point to a direct relationship between multinational economic organizations and ethnic response. The Brazilian case illustrates the need for organization, leadership, and resources to mobilize the aggrieved community within a larger society. Class inequalities are not always sufficient to generate an ethno-nationalistic force.

Professors Fontaine and Hill analyze the challenge a foreign-based MNC poses to the economic and political sovereignty of once-colonial societies in the Caribbean: MNCs tend to reinforce the "cultural division of labor" inherited from colonial regimes.[5] They discovered that any real ethnic (racial) reaction was blunted by the indigenous governments.[6] Eventually, the ethnic (racial) distinctions played upon by the MNCs resulted in awareness and identification, thereby generating a basis for challenge. Since class differences persisted after independence, class consciousness alone was not sufficient to confront the MNCs. Rather, as documented here, ethnic (racial) identification provided the glue for a leadership to consolidate a response to both MNCs and compliant governments.

Fontaine and Hill examine the complexity of the political economy and the response of a Caribbean island. They provide concepts necessary for analyzing relationships among ethnicity or racial identification, the state, and the multinational economic order. Their analysis gives an excellent example of ethnic (racial) awareness as a base of legitimacy and organization.

The Caribbean study highlights differences between the old colonial trading company and the contemporary MNC. Trading companies of the past held special charters expropriated by force or by negotiation with indigenous rulers. These companies were agents of the colonial powers, operating for the elites of the "mother" countries. Operating either under the license or the direct supervision of a colonial power, they were an integral part of the colonial regime. Thus, only two levels of political dominance existed: the "colonizer" and the "colonized." The multinational corporation, on the other hand, confronts a more complex environment without *overt* license or protection from a mother country. The MNC must negotiate its presence with the host country. Fontaine and Hill describe in the Caribbean case that the aggrieved minorities may influence government policy through organization and protest. The host government, then, has become an intervening institution between the society and the forces of the international economic order.

The MNC of today has no alternative but to operate differently from the colonial trading company of the past. Contemporary national elites can use the state to moderate the impact of the international economy. The state's response, of course, is circumscribed by the resources of its multinational contenders and the susceptibility of part or all of the elite to cooptation.

4

Professor Rawkins focuses on ethno-nationialism as a response to economic rationalism at the international level. The analysis is cast in the context of sociological—particularly Weberian—theory. Rawkins reminds the reader that ethnic identification and ethno-nationalism are not unique to the Third World, but are prevalent in Western Europe and North America. Moreover this study emphasizes that ethno-nationalism is an emotional response to economic and political forces. Economics of scale may reduce external competition and maximize economic security. In this sense, the European Economic Community serves its member nations well. Rawkins argues, however, that in the process of rationalization and bureaucratization, individual and collective identities are threatened. Through cultural attachments such as ethnic identification, meaningful communication is reestablished, fulfilling human moral and spiritual needs.[7]

Rawkins incorporates a "functionalist" explanation for the reemergence of ethnic identity in the industrial state and the world economy. Ethnic identification fulfills a psychological need created by impersonal forces of economic change and rationalization of everyday life. His analysis goes beyond the functionalist theory. Rawkins strongly suggests that ethno-nationalism fulfills a need for *gemeinshaft,* legitimizing a reaction to the prevailing "cultural division of labor."[8] In the West European case, such division is reinforced by the European Economic Community and the multinational corporation.

The four studies raise a number of important points regarding the relationship between ethnicity and international economic developments. Human organization takes many forms, operates to pursue different goals, and derives justification from varying needs and desires. Conflicts between ethnicity and the multinational corporation highlight one expression of that diversity.

5

FOOTNOTES

1. This conference was sponsored and organized by the Comparative Studies Program, Undergraduate Component, of the University of Denver and funded by a grant from OE/HEW to the University of Denver's Graduate School of International Studies. All opinions expressed in this monograph are the sole responsibility of the contributors and editors.

2. "Center-periphery cleavage" is a concept well-known in the literature on ethnicity and class conflict and yet is narrowly confined to this one area of academic inquiry. An early explanation of the phrase is available in Seymour M. Lipset and Stein Rokkan, eds., *Party Systems and Voter Alignments,* New York: Free Press, 1967, "Introduction." Use of the concept in this monograph relies heavily upon its further development and clarification by Michael Hechter, *Internal Colonialism: The Celtic Fringe in British National Development, 1536-1966,* Berkeley: U. of Cal. Press, 1975.

3. The levels of political organization refer to relationships distributed across socio-political space and across the more familiar terrain of geography and history. The temporal order of events and the physical location of actors involved are inadequate. In this case, we focus on the "political" dimension in analyzing the relationship between ethnicity and international economic organizations.

4. Papers presented in the first panel are not included here. However, they set the background for presentation and discussion of those printed in this volume. They include: Pierre van den Bergh, "Nigeria and Peru: Two Contrasting Cases in Ethnic Pluralism," published in *International Journal of Comparative Sociology* (in press); Eric Nordlinger, "Military Governments in Communally Divided Societies: Their Impact Upon National Integration," extracted from Chapter II of his book, *Soldiers and Politics: Military Coups and Movements,* New York: Prentice-Hall, 1977; and John Grove, "Ethnic and Racial Socio-Economic Inequality: Some Cross-National Evidence."

5. Hechter created the phrase "cultural division of labor," which succinctly captures an encompassing type of human inequality. He explains:

> The spatially uneven wave of modernization over state territory creates relatively advanced and less advanced groups. As a consequence of this initial fortuitious advantage, resources and power between the two groups are unequally distributed. The superordinate group, or core, seeks to stabilize and modernize its advantages through policies aimed at the institutionalization of the existing stratification system. It attempts to regulate the allocation of social roles so that those commonly defined as having high prestige are reserved for its members. Conversely, individuals from the less advanced group are denied access to these roles.

See Michael Hechter, *Internal Colonialism,* Berkeley: U. of Calif. Press, 1975:9.

6. In the studies presented in this monograph, there is no reason to treat *racial* identification and racially motivated nationalism as separate from *ethnic* identification and ethno-nationalism. For those who argue a fundamental distinction between race and ethnicity, there are a host of examples available for the counter argument. At the

core of this issue is whether social discrimination is based upon "real" or perceived differences between persons, and the obvious response is that everything is perceived.

7. Rawkins admits something is changing in modern societies, but he rejects by implication that the sort of change and usual accompanying conflict is applicable only to societies in one development stage. He argues that man not only has, but needs "primordial attachments," cultural "givens" of social existence, and he therefore is challenging such social theorists as Clifford Geertz. See "The Integrative Revolution: Primordial Sentiments and Civil Politics in the New States," in Clifford Geertz, ed., *Old Societies and New States: The Quest for Modernity in Asia and Africa*, New York: Free Press, Glencoe, Ill., 1963, especially p. 108. Setting the tempo of the 1950s and 1960s to understand social and political process in the new states, Geertz expresses the idea that non-modern society confronts emotional problems of human identification that industrialized societies have overcome. Rawkins' response is that "primordial sentiments" are part of man's nature and play a role in the continual processes of the rationalization and anonymous emotional, collective responses by those not immediately benefiting by such change.

8. For a discussion of the "functionalist" theory of ethnic change and conflict and a counter-thesis of a "reactive" theory, see Hechter, *op.cit.,* especially pp. 312-17. In contemporary social science fashion, Hechter builds his argument by operating on a dichotomy.

7

MULTINATIONAL CORPORATIONS IN THE MAKING AND UNMAKING OF ETHNIC GROUPS

Cynthia H. Enloe

Introduction

Modern companies have shaped ethnic identities and inter-ethnic distributions of power in six principal ways: (1) by "opening" ethnically distinct territories to new contacts with other groups; (2) by recruitment policies which deliberately have attracted members of certain ethnic groups either to or away from a region; (3) by reinforcing or diluting existing inter-ethnic differences through in-plant differentiation; (4) by providing some groups more than others with resources that could be utilized in political competition; (5) by altering the intra-communal distribution of status and rewards so as to change communal class structures; and (6) by affecting the international role of the nation-state which one ethnic group might dominate.

Multinational corporations do all of these things, but their prime distinctiveness lies in the particular impact they have on resource imbalance and the international role of the nation-state. Multinational corporations, even more than their economic precursors, affect the distribution of power within a political system relative to the various ethnic groups, and shape the uses to which a national political structure can be put if controlled by one community. The emergence of MNCs, furthermore, has made an effectively centralized nation-state authority appear all the more necessary in the latter half of the twentieth century, and centralizing authorities typically are impatient with subnational ethnic fragmentations, even while their own actions often exacerbate inter-ethnic tensions and mobilize individuals around ethnic loyalties.

The following discussion is based on incomplete data and tentative interpretations, but it is intended to raise the question: Just how new is the multinational corporation and just how new is the New International Economic Order (NIEO), both viewed ethnically? In thinking about multinational corporations and ways for ordering international economic and political relations, certain operational dynamics of the system have shown some consistency over time. This is *not* to suggest that MNCs have had no serious effects nor that the NIEO does not portend radical alterations in power relationships. But basic conditions that give rise to ethnicity may be independent from MNC activity. If this is possible—that the distributions of international economic power can undergo basic change without seriously altering inter-ethnic relations—it would mirror several prominent revolutions in Russia, China, and France,

9

where radical change occurred but critical inter-ethnic power relationships persisted.[1]

MNCs in the International Economic System

The basic condition that the NIEO is intended to alter is the inequality between industrialized countries and those countries which rely on exportation of raw materials for their income. This inequity existed long before the multinational corporation emerged as the prevalent enterprise form. Colonialism depended upon the existence of trading companies, plantation companies, and extractive firms owned and controlled in the colonizing nation, yet extending their operations abroad in the colonies. There may be less to the uniqueness of the MNC than meets the eye. MNCs remain essentially one-country owned, no matter how nationally diverse their branch offices and executives may be. What is distinctive about MNCs is their operation in countries that are nominally sovereign and their diversification of functions. Whereas the imperialist companies operating abroad were overwhelmingly involved in agricultural production and natural resource extraction, today they are involved as well in manufacturing. In addition, the MNCs increasingly perceive the peoples of the poor countries not just as passive bystanders or cheap labor, but as potential consumers of their processed goods.

What makes the earlier overseas firms and what we now call multinational corporations so similar with regard to ethnic effect is their labor policies. If we look at past and present overseas firms from the vantage point of labor, there is a striking similarity between them in the advantages they derived from the asymmetrical international order. Both forms of enterprise saw the benefits of employing manpower from outside the nation that served as their base of ownership and executive control. Nor was it just a matter of making use of the labor pool closest at hand—that is, recruiting laborers in the vicinity of the company's particular overseas plantation or mining operation—for both past and present overseas firms deliberately recruited unskilled labor from great distances if the labor they found close to the plantation or mining site was deemed somehow unsuitable by the management.

In terms of the international order in the colonial and post-colonial eras, such labor practices had several important effects. First, they brought a growing number of the world's laborers into direct relationship of dependency on the international economic system.[2] A Tamil laborer working on a Ceylonese tea plantation is no less a part of the international economic order than is a Lipton Corporation shareholder in New York or London. Second, labor practices of these overseas firms perpetuated and usually exacerbated gaps between territorially defined groups or between the rich and the poor.

10

Third, past and present labor practices stimulated massive movements of labor through slavery, labor indenture, labor contracting, and emigration programs. These policies accentuated ethnic divisions in the country where the overseas firms established operations, and contributed to inter-ethnic inequities. The principal differences between older forms of overseas firms and multinational corporations are twofold. There are now more MNCs controlling an ever-expanding proportion of the world's total goods and services and, more importantly, multinational firms must deal with sovereign regimes rather than with dependencies. Do these factors make a difference? If one traces a firm that has had major operations abroad over the last century, including colonized areas that have become independent states, would one necessarily find major changes in the firm's labor practices and impact on inter-ethnic relationships? One could look at Bookers, for example, a sugar company in Guyana, (formerly British Guiana) from the mid-1800s through the turbulent first years of independence up to the present, when Bookers is on the verge of being nationalized by the Guyanese PNC regime. Michelin rubber company policies in Indochina could be examined from French colonization through wars of liberation to the current period of Communist regimes in its three nation-state parts. A strong thread of consistency on labor practices and manipulations of ethnic categories over time might be discovered. Significant changes that had occurred would have originated outside the firm; war, independence, regime change, nationalization procedures, and interruption of migration flows may cause companies to modify employment policies. Even these political changes, however, do not inevitably alter fundamental labor practices and ethnic group relationships.

One study which focuses on Africa used two basic criteria to define multinational corporations: the firms operate in two or more countries, with assets—usually twenty percent or more—distributed among at least two states. To be genuinely multinational, however, a company must be characterized by a "substantial international dispersion of the firm's total assets" among several, not just two, countries.[3] During the colonial era, imperialist companies typically operated in several areas abroad that were controlled by the home state. Yet the last three decades of decolonization have broken down imperial fences so that western and Japanese firms now set up operations in what used to be other states' bailiwicks. This has permitted spread and diversification of multinational corporations. Such proliferation does not mean necessarily that MNCs are pursuing labor and ethnic policies basically different from those of earlier firms.

What may be more significant is the move of MNCs into overseas manufacturing, away from the colonial inclination to specialize abroad in agricultural and extractive operations. Multinationals' manufacturing operations share certain characteristics: they are usually capital intensive (even though they may have moved the firm's factories overseas, attracted there by cheap labor); they are urban oriented; they drive out smaller local firms which lack comparable access to capital and technology; and, typically, they establish political links to local elites. Insofar as MNCs are involved in overseas manufacturing, they are new, but, once again, their newness may not be as important in labor and ethnic terms as first appears. Even MNCs manufacturing in several countries may simply reinforce certain labor and ethnic imbalances created by the older type of overseas firm. In addition, they may exacerbate labor-ethnic problems in their home base society that have roots in much earlier enterprise practices.

Overseas firm operations began to have an impact on labor and communal relationships before the 1960s. What is new is the visibility of the dysfunctional character of those impacts to organized labor in the home base country. Much of what is written about the labor consequences of MNCs today does not concern workers in overseas operations, but focuses on negative impacts on the workers in the corporations' country of origin, particularly unemployment and wage depression.[4]

MNCs and Ethnic Selectivity

Multinational corporations usually are associated with the forces of modernization because they are—especially in their manufacturing branches—capital intensive, urban-oriented and cosmopolitan. Furthermore, they are organized on rational lines of impersonal functional divisions of labor. One influential cross-national study of conditions that enhance modern attitudes among men (women were not studied), Alex Inkeles' and David Smith's *Becoming Modern,* concludes that although schooling is still most powerful, the factory runs a close second. In all six countries surveyed, men who had worked in factories were more likely to hold ideas and behave in ways that were distinctively modern.[5] Inkeles and Smith did not specify supra-ethnic identification as one of the key ingredients of modern behavior, but that certainly has been the strong presumption of observers delineating modernity's peculiar modality.

If multinational corporations are the "engines of change"—whether that change be evaluated as increasing development or increasing underdevelopment (Rostow versus Frank, for example)—are they affecting change in sub-national communal attachments so as to diminish traditional ethnic loyalties? If the past practices of overseas firms are any guide, they are not. Colonial firms, as well as industries concentrated in a single western country,

12

have consciously employed ethnic categories in hiring, promoting, and assigning functions. These firms, in their own time, were also considered forces for modernization. In fact, their utilization of ethnic categories was part of their effort to be modern, to maximize efficiency, and to optimize labor resources. If firms we now label multinational corporations function any less ethnically, we will have to be able to cite explicit reasons for such a change. In other words, a basis must exist to assume that MNCs operate without using ethnic categories in hiring practices rather than presuming they are like their early modern precursors in making ethnic calculations.

Several illustrations may demonstrate how and why early overseas firms found ethnicity so functional. Tamara Hareven, an historian investigating how family organization was effected by industrialization, found that the large textile mills of Manchester, New Hampshire, used ethnicity to recruit industrial workers and bind them to the firm. The Amoskeag industries' managers made deliberate use of the then-most-up-to-date management techniques of the Taylor School when they decided that French-Canadians made particularly good workers for their mills. Furthermore, the in-factory stratification and divisions of labor were organized so as to play on the workers' ethnic feelings for the sake of heightening worker satisfaction and loyalty to the firm. Outside the plant, the company conducted recruitment programs in Quebec to bring French-Canadian families to Manchester; once they arrived, their housing tracts became ethnic neighborhoods. When their presumably loyal French-Canadian mill workers went on strike in the 1920s, the industrial managers reassessed their ethnic-industrial strategy. Deciding the community they considered ideal for mill work was not so ideal after all, they determined other ethnic groups should be brought into the mills.[6] Hiring criteria remained focused on ethnic categories.

Reading Hareven's studies, one is struck by how analogous this sort of ethnic strategizing is to ethnic calculating among early modern military organizers, for the military commanders and their civilian superiors also thought in ethnic terms when trying to predict what type of men would make the best recruits for their operations.[7] There is a striking similarity between the "martial race" concept and the "industrial race" formula. In each instance, organizational managers set about recruiting men who would be hardworking (at machines or in the trenches) and politically reliable. Gross group labeling rather than individual aptitude measurement is still used by managers of complex firms who worry about recruiting hundreds of workers in their continual search for rough formulas to insure there will not be rapid turnover or open defiance. Behavior predictability is a critical good in any modern organization, and ethnic categories are still relied upon to optimize it in economic enterprises and in military organizations.

13

In underdeveloped countries modern firms also used ethnicity for recruitment and in-plant organization. European plantation managers in Indonesia, for instance, relied heavily on imported labor as well as imported capital and food, particularly on those plantations where the local inhabitants' ethnic attributes did not seem, in the eyes of the planters, to make them available and/or reliable workers. In the East Coast Regency of Sumatra, tea, coffee, rubber, and palm oil plantations were set among inhabitants who were living well enough not to be attracted by the wage labor the planters offered. Planters imported their labor first from China, and then, as Chinese moved into commerical enterprises of their own, from Java. This obviously changed the ethnic balance in Sumatra, with long term communal and political consequences for Indonesia.[8] Similarly in Guyana after slavery was abolished (Africans were imported originally because the Dutch and English found the local AmerIndians too few in number and not suitable for plantation work), the sugar companies shopped around the globe for workers to replace the Africans who had left the sugar cane fields for villages of their own. After trying Portuguese and Chinese, they hit upon East Indians. Today more than fifty percent of Guyana's population is East Indians who still make up the overwhelmingly majority of estate workers.

Companies now labeled "multinationals" because they operate in independent states rather than in colonies continue to have significant impacts on ethnic group orientations and inter-ethnic relations. In Indonesia, corporations based in the United States, Europe, Canada, and Japan are intensifying inter-ethnic contacts between Indonesian subgroups by opening new operations—mainly extractive—in the outer islands, beyond central Java. Sulawesi-Javanese group relations, for example, are affected when International Nickel (INCO) decides that its Canadian sources are running low and discovers likely deposits in Sulawesi.[9] This INCO venture does not simply increase the level of interactions between Sulawesi and Javanese, but affects the dominant Javanese group's ability to penetrate the Sulawesi area. The Javanese control the central government, and the government works closely with INCO (and other multinational firms) to accelerate economic growth through extension of centrally controlled infrastructures.

In a similar fashion, the British-Canadian corporation, the Hudson's Bay Company, is a vehicle for increasing and sustaining the penetration of South Africa's Afrikaner community into the territory of the Ovambo people of Namibia. Dealing in the high-demand karakul sheep fur, the Hudson's Bay Company has agreements with Afrikaner farmers in Namibia who in turn depend largely on Ovambo laborers hired under restrictive contracts.[10] To explain the inter-African as well as inter-racial relations currently shaping the political conflict in Namibia, then, one must talk about the ethnic consequences of the multinational Hudson's Bay Company operations in Namibia. It would be as unrealistic to try to analyze the history of ethnic politics in northern Canada between whites and native Canadian-Americans while omitting the critical role played by the Hudson's Bay Company, then based and owned in London, as it would be to omit the company from the post-colonial Namibian ethnic equation today.

The multinational corporations' role is often conceded to be one of enhancing national integration, of intensifying the penetration of ruling groups into sectors previously enjoying considerable autonomy. It is assumed at the same time that multinationals, by introducing technology and expanding modern sector job opportunities, will lessen inter-ethnic barriers on a personal level. Unfortunately, we have all too few studies of inter-ethnic relations within plants. The hiring and retention strategies mentioned above suggest that in reality corporate managers may find ethnic divisions functional and worth maintaining. Fred von der Mehden, for example, in his work on foreign electronics companies in Penang, Malaysia, found that within the factories managers had come to organize work sections by ethnic groups, so that all Malay women sat in one area, all Chinese women in another, each with immediate supervisors from their own language group.[11]

Other conditions may also affect the inability of multinationals to enhance ethnic integration. For example, different cultural attitudes that workers bring to the workplace with them stem largely from ethnic differences. And, differences in skill access between various ethnic communities in any country playing host to multinationals will partially determine hiring patterns.

A provocative study has been conducted in Thailand among Thai and Thai-Chinese employees in modern sector firms, including branches of MNCs. The study does not isolate the impact of MNC working conditions, but it does suggest that MNCs and modern sector local commerical firms may have a similiar effect on ethnic amalgamation. In his imaginative survey of the work attitudes of white-collar workers in Thailand, Frederic C. Deyo found that there was a clear distinction between Thai and Thai-Chinese workers' personal notions of job satisfaction, career prospects, and on-the-job status relations. Even more striking, though, was his discovery that there were major differences between Thai men and Thai women workers and especially between Thai-Chinese men and Thai-Chinese women workers. For instance, his interviews revealed that Thai-Chinese women were considerably more ambitious and saw job rewards in terms of getting ahead in the company; their male counterparts cared more about cultivating friendships on the job and using job rewards to permit them to cultivate out-of-work interests.[12] Deyo suggests, then, that MNCs and other modern sector firms just provide a new setting for sex as well as ethnic differences to be expressed. Persons employed in modern sector firms may have to adopt certain standard behavior patterns with regard to scheduling of time or synchronization of work, but they are not merely ciphers; they bring cultural preconceptions and values with them and use them at work.

The unequal distribution of skills that MNCs look for in their employees obviously affects ethnic composition of the corporate work force. If workers in the MNC sector of any multi-ethnic country's economy are disproportionately from one community, this either offsets imbalances between ethnic groups in politics, or, as is more likely, accentuates imbalances that already exist in other areas of national life. Language skills are among the most prominent in determining who will be hired by multinationals involved in manufacturing. Literacy or knowledge of a European language is less important in operating a mine or plantation. In agricultural and extractive enterprises, the MNC managers may be more concerned with those allegedly ethnic qualities of hard work and dependability of their predecessors. But as MNCs move into manufacturing and processing abroad, these maldistributions of foreign language facility and literacy play a growing part in widening gaps between already unequal ethnic groups.

One can see this situation in Singapore among Singapore Chinese, Indians, and Malays. Although the Peoples Action Party (PAP) regime of Lee Juan Hew enunciates a policy of equity among the four languages spoken by the island-nation's different communities, English is the dominant language in commerce in large part because of MNC reinforcement of British colonial trading patterns. Neither the majority Chinese community (seventy-six percent of the population), nor the Indians (seven percent), nor the politically significant Malay minority (fifteen percent), are native English speakers; each group has public schools in its own language. But Indians and Chinese have outpaced the Malays in acquiring English language skills. According to a recent study of language facility among Singaporeans, the Indians, perhaps because of their otherwise marginal status, revealed seventy percent oral-aural competence in English, while Chinese were next best with twenty-three percent. Malays lagged behind with only nineteen percent.[13] Furthermore, because there are Taiwan and Hong Kong Chinese multinationals operating in Singapore, there is at least the chance that a Chinese-speaking Chinese without English competence could be employed in the foreign economic sector, whereas there are few Malay overseas firms in Singapore to provide jobs for Malay-speaking Malays. Because the foreign sector has become so

16

important to overall development strategy in Singapore, the Malay lag in acquiring language skills that give them access to this sector is a factor in widening ethnic differentials regardless of official PAP pronouncements.

MNCs and Ethnic Labor Politicization

Some employment policies of multinational corporations may have unintended effects on ethnic relations. Just as infantry recruitment from one "reliable" ethnic community can lead to future mobilization around grievances, such as mutiny, hiring a labor force largely from one ethnic group may at some future date allow for worker organization and even strikes.[14] If a mutiny or strike occurs, the commanders or managers usually follow a two stage course of action, once they recover from their initial feeling of being "betrayed" by their ranks. First, they are likely to enlist workers or troops of deliberately different ethnic identity to act as scabs or mutiny suppressors. That is, the ethnic homogeneity of the discontented ranks prompts an ethnic response by those in charge. Once order is restored, superiors reassess earlier ethnic recruitment strategies. Communal traits they assumed made good soldiers or workers are rejected; new traits are substituted. In the wake of the militancy, then, there is apt to be a change in communal recruitment patterns and a change in superiors' ethnic stereotypings. Post-strike or post-mutiny recruitment may be deliberately multi-ethnic in order to deprive future workers of those communally-derived assets useful for mobilization, or recruitment may be again distinctly mono-ethnic, but with the ethnic ideal switched from one group to another.

The phenomenon described here—worker actions and managerial response—is not peculiar to overseas firms; it exists among exclusively domestic companies where the labor pool is divided ethnically. But it would seem MNCs rarely break this pattern. Their workers have been among those to draw upon communal ties in order to organize and strike, pressing for their own interests.

A surprising incident occurred in England recently, in which an ethnically distinctive work force organized a strike against a multinational corporation. In mid-1974, Asian women workers (primarily Indians) who made up the major component of the Imperial Typewriter factory force in Leicester went out on an unauthorized strike to protest the multinational firm's decision to close the factory. The management argued that Imperial Typewriter sales were not adequate in Britain to justify a factory operation. The women's union, the national union, and the government's Department of Employment were surprised by the women's militancy. The union hierarchy, overwhelmingly white, male and British-born, tried to dampen rather than to assist the strikers.[15] It was probably presumed that workers—female, Asian, immigrants—would be pliant and unlikely to protest, even when foreign corporate decisions were about to eliminate their jobs. A victory for the Asian women workers was achieved: the Imperial management agreed not to close the factory at that time. But ethnic consequences went beyond the Imperial Typewriter plant. Imperial employees became important supporters for Asian women workers who, six months later, staged a one-day strike at the Leicester Kenilworth Components factory, demanding improved pay and a reduction in their long hours. Most of the women were Gujarati.[16]

Ethnically-based workers' organizations have been formed within other multinational firms—among Tamils on the British-owned Brooke-Bond tea plantation in Sri-Lanka; among East Indian workers on the British-owned Bookers sugar plantation in Guyana; among Afro-Guyanese bauxite workers on Alcan's Guyana bauxite company; among Afro-Trinidadian workers in the Shell Oil operations in Trinidad; and among Ovambo contract laborers in the Hudson's Bay Company fur operations in Namibia.[17]

The ethnic character of work forces in multinationals can also suppress worker organization and militancy. This has been the prediction upon which managers have based many of their recruitment strategies. First, the ethnic group that makes up the majority of the plantation, factory, or mine employees may be a group extremely vulnerable economically and politically, and restricted in the kind of concerted action it can afford to undertake. This is particularly true when the group is composed of immigrants who feel vulnerable due to host population hostility and the legal tenuousness of their employment status. Consequently, there have been relatively few effective worker organizations or strikes among the millions of foreign workers in locally-owned or foreign-owned enterprises in Western Europe. Second, the work force in a single plant may not be ethnically homogeneous except on a department by department basis, and in this case, the very things that build worker trust among employees of identical ethnic background within one division can serve to abort interdepartmental worker cooperation. This barrier is not immovable, but lowering it may mean overcoming ethnic suspicions. A Turkish woman who led a strike at the Eles stocking factory near Wiesbaden in West Germany told one researcher after the strike:

> But among us, who are striking, we have learnt a lot. When we came out
> on strike, we consisted of many different nationalities. We were Turks or
> Italians, or Greeks or Yugoslavs or Germans. But today we know that we
> all are just workers and that we have a common struggle to win. . .[18]

Among the countries where multinational corporations stand out visibly on the political-economic landscape are the oil-producing states of the Middle

East. MNCs in the Middle East, especially in the Gulf states, rely heavily on immigrant laborers. These workers are perceived by local Arabs as ethnically distinct, though in many cases they may be Muslim. Omanis reportedly resented the fact that Shell Oil Corporation, the principal source of Oman's revenue and employment, brought in Indian, Pakistani, and Iranian workers to fill its expanding payroll.[19] Joseph Kraft described the increasingly multi-ethnic and stratified character of the work force in Saudi Arabia caused by the recruitment policies of both the local regime and of the foreign corporations:

> Much of the heavy or dirty labor is done by immigrants (chiefly from Yemen), who come under contract for assigned jobs to be completed in limited periods. Palestinians and Egyptians do much of the office work, Syrians and Lebanese a good deal of the trading. The "guest workers" are said to number about a million. The native work force is truly miniscule—probably about five hundred thousand. . . . The new five year plan calls for bringing in six hundred thousand additional workers. . . .[20]

Workers imported under these controlled conditions, likely to be cut off from indigenous workers and stratified ethnically among themselves, cannot organize easily. While the ethnic make-up of overseas firms' work forces can and has encouraged worker mobilization, there are many factors hampering such concerted action and bolstering managers' confidence in utilizing an ethnic shorthand to recruit and control employees.

As it has been in the past, ethnicity is a two-edged sword, both enhancing and hindering mobilization. What the spread of multinational corporations does is *sharpen* each side of that sword. MNCs are a major factor increasing ethnic pluralism and inter-ethnic competition. At the same time, MNCs are a key factor in linking all sectors of a nation's economy. The MNCs, then, make worker cooperation across industries all the more crucial if worker impact is to be genuinely effective.

MNCs and Ethnic Political Regimes

We have emphasized primarily the effect of multinationals on ethnic-labor relationships in plural societies. But the labor consequences of multinationals have a ripple effect far beyond the workers employed by the firm itself.[21] They can shape the economic stratification system that determines distribution of power and rewards in the entire political system.

No central political regime is unmindful of that ripple effect. What differs is the capacity and the will of a given regime to intervene, limit, or redirect the ramifications. If a regime governs an ethnically divided polity and uses one ethnic group as its power base, it will attempt to influence multinational firm practices to lessen inter-ethnic antagonism or perhaps to strengthen the position of its own communal base relative to others which serve as potential bases for political challengers.

Is it possible to talk about ethnic politics—which frequently means *the politics*—of fragmented states without analyzing the role of the MNCs and their locally resident managers? Yes, apparently it is. In the literature on some of the prominent multi-ethnic states one finds little detail concerning the impact of MNCs on inter- or intra-ethnic politics. Yet to produce a *realistic* politically meaningful analysis of such systems, the multinational corporations' roles can no more be omitted than can U.S. Steel be neglected in a serious study of ethnic and racial politics in Gary, Indiana. For example, multinational corporations should be treated explicitly (even if their role is minimal) in studies of the ethnic political economics of Scottish-English relations in Britain, Christian-Muslim relations in Lebanon, Hausa-Yuroba-Ibo relations in Nigeria, Afrikaner-English-African relations in South Africa, and French-English relations in Canada.

There are presently some four hundred U.S.-owned multinational corporations that use Brussels as their European headquarters. The Belgian political system is shaped by two conditions: its role as center of the EEC, which in turn makes it an ideal site for MNCs, and the division between Walloons and Flemings which jeopardizes its political stability. In most analyses there is a tendency to treat U.S. citizens and other foreigners in Brussels and the companies they represent as non-actors, as analytically invisible or irrelevant. In much the same way, Europeans, Americans, and Japanese serving with MNCs are rarely referred to in standard analyses of Singapore's ethnic politics. In the common "census politics" that ethnic analysts undertake, these MNC employees appear only as marginal "others" or as unanalyzed background scenery.

In Belgium, however, MNCs' decisions regarding investment, intra-country site location, and labor recruitment *do* have profound impacts on the distribution of power among the local communities. Until World War II, the French-speaking Walloons in the south dominated the Belgian political and economic systems, but during the 1950s and 1960s, the coal and steel industries in Wallonia declined. At the same time, with General Motors in the lead, the great bulk of American investment was directed to Flanders, especially in and near the major Flemish port of Antwerp. This was a critical factor in shifting the balance from the Walloons to the Flemings, a shift which intensified inter-communal partisan conflict and eventually undermined the regime's stability.[22] To talk about growing tensions between the Walloons and Flemings with reference only to birth rates and political party splits, and to make no mention of General Motors, Monsanto, and Chemical Bank of New

York, is to leave a gaping hole in our understanding of ethnic politics in Belgium.[23]

It was mentioned earlier that MNCs and earlier forms of overseas firms have important attributes in common, but one of their principal differences is that multinationals have to deal with nominally sovereign governments. Their antecedents dealt mainly with colonial administrators. This change does not mean, however, that there will be an alteration of ethnic relationships. There are two circumstances that suggest how the shift from colonial to independent states affects the impact of a MNC on a society.

The first case consists of a post-colonial regime dominated by one ethnic group. Governmental leaders are more concerned with bolstering that group's position than with narrowing intercommunal gaps. The MNCs find themselves dealing with an ethnic leadership when neglecting licenses, tax incentives, exploration rights, and so on. The ethnic elite, on the other hand, takes steps to insure that its political hegemony is reinforced by shaping overseas investments and MNC local practices. This political advantage will be particularly pronounced if the regime moves to create national planning boards, nationalized trading corporations, or petroleum licensing corporations which heighten MNCs' dependency on the favor of the ruling communal leadership.

The MNCs may not find such a situation burdensome; it can make bargaining easier, *quid pro quos* become more predictable. The MNC advances its interests by working with the central elite to expand operations in new untapped regions of the country, while the central leadership uses the MNCs to penetrate and exert central planning authority into groups that heretofore had been beyond the reach of effective control. Such a situation exists in Indonesia today. Since the 1965 *coup*, the Javanese have bolstered and expanded their already notable dominance over the country's political economy and over non-Javanese communities.[24] Djakarta's Javanese-led bureaucracy uses the infrastructure of corporations to increase the hold over outer islands and to press foreign firms to follow the new laws restricting the Chinese minority's economic role. Multinational corporations in Japan, Europe, and North America consider Indonesia currently one of the most attractive places for foreign investment.

In a more graphic manner, multinational corporations serve to bolster the Afrikaner ruling group in South Africa. British and U.S. corporate investments have been growing in South Africa, despite the signs of strain and anxiety in that asymmetrical multi-ethnic system. Ford Motor Company and General Motors have been manufacturing cars in South Africa since the 1920s, lured, like other foreign firms, by political stability (in the form of the

21

Afrikaner-led Nationalist Party), by a convertible hard currency, by an abundance of cheap labor, and by a large domestic market coupled with access to other markets nearby. Although MNC executives contend they pay the highest wages to African workers and that *apartheid* would persist even if they all terminated their South African operations, it remains true that technology and economic growth made available largely through such foreign firms (including multinational banks) have given the Afrikaner community two things critical to the preservation of its communal dominance. First, it has made South Africa the leading industrial center and source of investment capital in southern Africa. This, in turn, has enabled the Nationalist regime to bargain with the dependent Black governments bordering South Africa to reduce external pressures against *apartheid*. Second, more recently, it has enabled the Afrikaners to move out of their formerly politically oriented role to exercise more leverage in the modern economic sector. As politics and economics become intimately intermeshed in South Africa, MNCs find it wise to reduce their traditional bias in favor of English South Africans and to provide more access to rising Afrikaner whites, adding new substance to Afrikaner power and tying whites of both ethnic groups more closely together.[25]

The South African and Indonesian cases illustrate that existing ethnic dominance is reinforced by MNC behavior. In each instance there is evidence that MNCs are used by central elites (often willingly) to alter ethnic stratifications—limiting local Chinese commercial activities in Indonesia, for example, or lessening English South Africans' economic preeminence in South Africa. In some countries, central regimes have made MNCs key instruments for basic change in ethnic relationships. In Brazil, multinational corporations play a strategic part in determining what sectors of the population will benefit from the country's much-publicized rapid rise in GNP. Brazil is pluralistic. In recognition of the inequities in that pluralism, the Brazilian government has passed laws prohibiting discrimination against Black Brazilians in hiring and promotion. Pierre-Michel Fontaine conducted a study of reactions by multinational corporations to those anti-discrimination laws. He concludes that while multinationals, especially those with experience in coping with U.S. anti-discrimination laws, may be particularly adept in avoiding blatant bias in their personnel practices, they generally follow Brazilian firms' practice of not assigning much weight to the laws. According to Fontaine, "ascriptive behavior, perhaps in some cases bordering on paternalism, is alive and well in the modern, cosmopolitan and achievement-oriented multinational corporation."[26] He found that Afro-Brazilians were concentrated at the lowest rungs of company ladders, with only a few visible at the middle levels, with "nary an African executive in sight, except for a very few management trainees in such huge firms as Volkswagen."[27] More basic than multinational corporations' compliance with specific laws intended to reduce inter-ethnic discrepancies is the multinational executives' adoption of the widespread myth held by Brazilians themselves concerning ethnic-racial relations in the country. MNC executives have decided to share in the belief that there are not genuine ethnic and racial divisions in Brazil. Adopting this view, Fontaine found, allowed the foreign executives and the Brazilians working in MNCs to act as if there were no problem and therefore no need for deliberate corporate action.[28]

In political systems where there is genuine interest in fundamentally altering ethnic power relationships, MNCs may have to respond to more serious pressures to hire and to promote members of weaker communities. In both Malaysia and in the Canadian province of Quebec, ethnically-based party regimes are attempting to rearrange economic stratifications. MNCs and local firms are urged to hire and to promote Malays in Malaysia and French-speaking Canadians in Quebec. Because MNCs represent the most powerful firms in the most rapidly growing sectors of each economy, the regimes' success in altering the corporations' behavior will determine the efficacy of the policy as a whole.

Malaysia's labor stratification along ethnic lines is as old as the British presence there. Indians were imported to man the British-owned rubber estates; Chinese were the manual laborers in both British and Chinese-owned tin mines and construction companies; in commerce, Chinese and Indians dominated smaller firms, while the largest trading companies were British. Malays remained predominantly rural, cultivating small rice and rubber holdings. When Malays did migrate to the cities for employment, they entered the military or the civil service where posts were reserved for them.[29] The tri-communal Alliance party (renamed the National Front to incorporate more parties) began to take serious steps to alter this employment-income pattern after the Malay-initiated riots in Kuala Lumpur following the 1969 elections. The New Economic Plan of 1973 called for pursuing multinational investment more assiduously than ever in order to achieve rapid economic growth and diversification beyond the traditional revenue earners' tin and rubber. Simultaneously, the NEP set forth its intent to redistribute economic modern sector rewards so the Malays, forty-five percent of the population, would possess one-third of the country's modern sector jobs and ownership. A combination of British, Japanese, U.S., Singapore, and Hong Kong firms control approximately two-thirds of the nation's economic modern sector, a fact that must modify the conventional ethnic wisdom in Malaysia that "Malays control the government and Chinese control the economy."[30] The National Front had to insure that foreign companies adhered to the goals of the NEP if Malays were indeed to gain employment and ownership access.

Fred von der Mehden found in his survey of managers of overseas firms in Malaysia that they were sensitive to Kuala Lumpur's pressures and had made efforts to meet the Malay employment quota standards. This sensitivity stems from foreign managers' assessment that the Malaysian regime and its political climate in general are more hospitable to MNCs than are those in alternative Third World locations. Accordingly, it is worth their while to make political adjustments so long as they do not threaten basic profitability. Von der Mehden found that Chinese company officers were especially wary of seeming to take any part in politics because of the traditional suspicion in which Chinese businessmen have been held in Malaysia. Both Chinese and non-Chinese executives need to keep abreast of changing government policies, contracts, and project plans, but they do so through civil service and informal contacts that draw the least public notice.[31]

For their part, Malay elites have gained a markedly greater economic leverage in Malaysia because of the presence of the multinationals and because of the Malays' stronger position in the government after the 1969 riots. Although Malaysian elites of all communities are believers in the free enterprise strategy for development, leaders of UMNO, the Malay party in the alliance, have created public corporations through which natural resource and industrial planning now occurs. Furthermore, the Ministry of Finance, which traditionally was the perquisite of the Chinese partner in the regime, for the first time is headed by an UMNO politician. The Prime Minister has always been the UMNO leader. It is through these institutions that foreign companies must work. Malay leaders do not have to try to upset local Chinese businesses; they can rely on expansion of British, U.S., Dutch, and Japanese enterprises to offset the older Chinese economic power, and these companies must negotiate with Malay technocrats and Malay politicians.

Although Malaysia is known in Asia for its relatively low level of corruption, two recent corruption cases reveal the shift in ethnic economic power— at the elite levels though not at the mass level—in Malaysia. The most publicized was the case of Datuk Harun, a leading UMNO politician. He was convicted by a Malaysian court, despite his political status, in May 1976, for seeking bribes from the Hong Kong and Shanghai Bank, a British multinational bank that needed Harun's permission to build a large new office building. Harun sought the funds for the UMNO treasury.[32] That is, a multinational bank sought to expand its investments through favoring a Malay politician and a Malay party. In the second instance, reporters uncovered an apparent bribe by the U.S. aerospace corporation, Northrop, given to insure that the Royal Malaysian Air Force would choose its F-5 fighters over competing aircraft. The persons who acted as the strategic middlemen between Northrop and the government in the delicate negotiations turned out to

24

be mainly Malays who all had personal connections with government officials.[33] What is significant here is not the evidence of corruption but the indication of how economically important the *upper strata of Malays* have become because the central government is taking a more active and institutionalized role in economic planning and because the new economic actors most important in that development are non-Chinese multinationals sensitive to the National Front's ethnic objectives.

In Canada there has not been as dramatic a change in ethnic economic-political stratification. Nationwide, in fact, the French Canadian minority has been slipping because of the influx of other ethnic communities and the growing political importance of the western states where so much of Canada's valuable natural resources are located. In Quebec, though, there has been a change, insofar as the current provincial regime is responding to French-Canadian nationalist ferment, less in the old paternalist mode than in a new assertive fashion that actually seeks to give French-Canadians a greater stake in the modern sector of the economy. As in Malaysia, that sector is dominated by multinational firms, chiefly British and American.

Language has been the the focal point for ethnic-labor policy change in Quebec. An official investigation revealed that all French workers in Quebec typically have to communicate formally in English. By contrast, English-speakers who have to use French were primarily those in manual jobs. Most English-speakers who had to use French as part of their occupational duties only had to use it orally, not in writing and reading as did their French counterparts using English. Generally, the study found that "French is used most in material production and that English increases in use as activity requires communication with the public, work peers, suppliers, and administrators, especially if the communication is in written form."[34] Consequently, for a regime to alter the fundamental political-economy of ethnic relations in Quebec, pressure would have to be imposed on the major private employers—U.S. and British multinationals—to use French language more at the upper levels of the companies, giving French-speakers a better chance for promotions and influence.

Effective implementation of such a policy is hindered by several factors. First, this is only a provincial level policy, whereas the companies are national or international. Federal policy under the Liberal Party has pursued bilingualism, but chiefly in the areas of civil service and military employment, not in the corporate sector. Second, the companies, and to a very large extent the labor unions organizing many of those companies' workers, are led by English-speakers who would have natural ties to the English-speaking elite in the province. This is rather different than in Malaysia, where, except for

25

overseas Chinese firms, the large multinational corporations are not ethnically linked to any one of the three local ethnic communities. Third, immigration continues in Canada, further diluting French-speakers' leverage. The Quebec government has tried to limit that dilution by legally requiring all new immigrant children residing in the province who do not speak English as their native tongue to attend French-speaking schools. This is a realistic policy in light of the eventual diminution of French as a language of work and mobility, but it has aroused considerable resentment on the part of Italian, Greek, and other new immigrants in Quebec.

Conclusion: New International Economic
Order and Ethnic Fragmentation

The failure of decolonization and gross economic growth to bring a redistribution of wealth and influence in the world has prompted a profound rethinking of the meaning of "development" and of "power." Despite decolonization and rising GNPs, the spread of multinational corporations has been probably the single most salient factor in the failure to move toward international equity. Multinational corporations' ability to maximize profits in legally sovereign states as earlier overseas firms did in colonies, suggests that genuine independence calls for more than pulling down one flag and raising another. Furthermore, multinational corporations, through investment capital and access to sophisticated technology, have been able to raise a host country's GNP without translating it into increased international power or enhanced well-being for the host country's mass level population.

The New International Economic Order is a concept and a strategic formula for accomplishing what decolonization and gross economic growth have not accomplished. Multinational corporations are among the chief targets for change, though with a recognition that MNCs' advantages in the international economy depend largely on the support they receive from their respective home governments. At bottom, the NIEO intends to reduce the dependent status of those nations which currently rely on the export of raw materials for their revenues and whose smaller revenues from processed goods depend on the operations of foreign-owned companies. Although the intermediate objectives—such as commodity reserves, debt restructuring, and technology transfer—have been the focus of most of the negotiations at the meetings of the Group of 77 and have been emphasized by spokesmen for the Third World and at UNCTAD, the ultimate objective is to insure that Third World nations gain the opportunity to industrialize and to control their own industries. Only world-wide redistribution of industrialization can break the cycle of dependency in which nations exporting raw materials find themselves perpetually caught.[35]

26

Rarely are ethnic considerations introduced into the promotion *or* criticism of the New International Economic Order. Only when ethnic cleavages take the form of blatant racial stratification, as in southern Africa, are ethnically related questions posed. But both the multinational corporations and the NIEO alternative to dependence on multinationals have far-reaching consequences for ethnic identities and inter-ethnic distributions of power. Most of this paper has been devoted to demonstrating how MNCs, as much as earlier overseas firms, took explicit account of ethnic divisions in hiring and in internal divisions of labor. The most widespread result of overseas firms' operations was to widen the gap between weak and dominant communities and to exacerbate ethnic pluralism within a given country—within their home base country as well as in their foreign base of operations. Even when post-colonial independent regimes gained power, if they operated in a multi-ethnic state, the regimes were prone to be communally oriented. In their exertions of influence on multinationals, then, such regimes were apt to try to translate their political leverage into a confirmation of existing economic power or into the creation of new economic power for the single community.

If the NIEO is interpreted solely in nation-state terms, there is every likelihood that it may bring about a redistribution of influence between nations, without touching intra-national cleavages and inequities. If national regimes are taken as the substitutes for multinational corporations, not only may inter-ethnic gaps persist, but they may widen where the national regime is dominated by one ethnic group.

In the Group of 77 and UNCTAD discussions, national-level alterations attracted the most attention. However, in the dependency theorists' writings, more attention is devoted to *intra*-national cleavages mirroring international inequities since, as Andre Frank and others contend, class disparities have been created and sharpened within each Third World nation as cosmopolitan elites reap disproportionate benefits from the country's dependent relations with the industrialized states.[36] Quantitative investigations testing this theory—that increased national dependency produces widening intra-national class disparities—generally substantiate the contention.[37] Although dependency theorists talk mostly in terms of class divisions and are rather uncomfortable with the concept of ethnicity, their writings can be used to shed light on the implications of the NIEO.

If the operations of multinational corporations have helped perpetuate ethnic cleavages, and if in many countries multinationals' behavior has helped create or confirm the dominant position of one ethnic community over others, then NIEO strategies should act to reduce inter-ethnic disparities and hostilities.[38] This will occur, however, only if direct analysis is done on the ethnic

27

ramifications of multinational corporations' operations in ethnically fragmented societies and if steps taken to reduce MNCs' influence are monitored
at the ethnic and nation-state level.

FOOTNOTES

1. I attempted to analyze the degree of change produced by revolutions viewed from an ethnic perspective in Cynthia H. Enloe, *Ethnic Conflict and Political Development*, Boston: Little, Brown & Company, 1973, Chapter 9.

2. Karl Deutsch has contended that a *smaller* proportion of employed people in the world today are employed in the international sector than were employed in the 1920s. Presumably this is the result of decolonization. Karl W. Deutsch, "On Inequality and Limited Growth: Some World Politics Effects," *International Studies Quarterly*, Vol. 19, No. 4, December, 1975: 385.

3. U.N. Economic Commission for Africa, *The Multinational Corporations in Africa*, London: Rex Collins, 1972: 2.

4. For the distortive impact of multinational manufacturing operations on host Third World countries, see Steven Langdon, "Multinational Corporations, Taste Transfer and Underdevelopment: A Case Study from Kenya," *Review of African Political Economy*, No. 2, January-April 1975: 12-35. One of the best discussions of the effect of MNCs on home country labor is contained in Richard J. Barnet and Ronald Müller, *Global Reach*, New York: Simon and Schuster, 1974. An American labor union analyst's view is found in: Nat Weinberg, "The Multinational Corporation and Labor," in Abdul A. Said and Luiz R. Simmons, *The New Sovereigns*, Englewood Cliffs, N.J.: Prentice-Hall, 1975: 91-107.

5. Alex Inkeles and David Smith, *Becoming Modern*, Cambridge, Mass.: Harvard University Press, 1974.

6. Tamara K. Hareven, "The Laborers of Manchester, New Hampshire, 1912-1922: The Role of the Family and Ethnicity in Adjustment to Industrial Life," *Labor History*, Vol. 16, No. 2, Spring, 1975: 251-265.

7. For ethnic calculations in the organization of militaries, see Cynthia H. Enloe, "The Military Uses of Ethnicity," *Millenium* (London School of Economics), Vol. 4, No. 3, Winter, 1975-76: 220-234; Enloe, "Ethnic Factors in the Evolution of the South African Military," *Issue* (African Studies Association), Vol. 5, No. 4, Winter, 1975: 21-28; Eric Nordlinger, *Praetorian Soldiers*, unpublished manuscript, mimeo, Harvard University, 1975, Chapter 5; Warren Young, "Black, Brown, and Khaki: The New Commonwealth Immigrant and Her Majesty's Forces," in Cynthia H. Enloe and Ursula Semin-Panzer, eds., *The Military, The Police and Domestic Order*, London: Richardson Institute for Conflict and Peace Research, 1976.

8. Bob Catley, "The Development of Underdevelopment in Southeast Asia," *Journal of Contemporary Asia*, Vol. 6, No. 1, 1976: 58-59.

9. Development Education Centre, "Indonesia, Guatemala: INCO Plunders Third World," *Third World Forum*, Vol. 2, No. 1, November-December, 1975: 4-10.

10. Susan Hurlich, "Hudson's Bay Company: Enemy of Canada's Nature Peoples and Namibians," *Third World Forum*, Vol. 2, No. 1, November-December, 1975: 24-26.

11. Personal communication with Professor Fred von der Mehden, December, 1975.

12. Frederic C. Deyo, "Ethnicity and Work Culture in Thailand: A Comparison of Thai and Thai-Chinese White-Collar Workers," *Journal of Asian Studies,* Vol. 34, No. 4, August, 1975: 995-1016.

13. John A. MacDougall and Chew Sock Foon, "English Language Competence and Occupational Mobility of Singapore," *Pacific Affairs,* Summer, 1976: 294-312.

14. I am grateful to Professor Tamara Hareven for bringing to my attention the analogy between strikes and mutinies, personal communication. Cambridge, Mass., May, 1976.

15. "Kenilworth Strike Defeated," *Race Today,* December, 1974: 320.

16. *Loc. sit.*

17. For analyses of Tamil minority politics and the tea industry in Sri Lanka, see: John Hamilton *et al., Tea: The Colonial Legacy,* Cambridge, UK, Cambridge World Development Action Group, 1975. Regarding labor-ethnic divisions in Trinidad, there are now moves to build an alliance between the Afro-Trinidadian oil workers union and the East Indian-Trinidadian sugar cane workers union. See "A Working Class Party in Trinidad," *Race Today,* February, 1976: 33.

18. Godula Kosak, "Migrant Women: The Move to Western Europe—A Step Towards Emancipation?" *Race and Class,* Vol. 17, No. 4, Spring, 1976: 377. A perceptive description of both the ethnic and sex factors shaping the lives of Yugoslav workers in Sweden is: Jane Kramer, "Profiles: The Invandrare," *New Yorker,* March 22, 1976: 43-84. It is interesting to note that Eastern European states are also finding it necessary to import foreign workers. In 1976 there were a reported 10,000 foreign workers employed in Czechoslovakia, to which 3,600 Vietnamese workers have recently been added and 1,500 Greek Cypriot workers were soon to be added. *New York Times,* April 25, 1976.

19. *Christian Science Monitor,* October 5, 1971. I am indebted to Professor Ann Schulz of Clark University for pointing out the growing importance of immigrant workers in the Gulf states.

20. Joseph Kraft, "Letters from Saudi Arabia," *New Yorker,* October 20, 1975: 115.

21. Robert W. Cox, "Labor and the Multinationals," *Foreign Affairs,* January, 1976: 344-365.

22. Daniel Yergin, "Brussels," *The Atlantic,* June, 1976: 20.

23. It is only fair to acknowledge that in my own earlier attempt to analyze Belgian ethnic politics, I completely omitted any mention of multinational corporations. Enloe, *Ethnic Conflict and Political Development, op.cit.,* 118-121.

24. Derek Davies, "Bureaucratic Bottleneck in Indonesia," *Far Eastern Economic Review*, May 28, 1976: 103-106.

25. A discussion of U.S. corporate practices in South Africa is contained in Ovid Demaris, *Dirty Business*, New York: Avon Books, 1974: 154-155; the inherent contradictions between economic modernization and apartheid with regard to White dependency or African labor are analyzed in Herbert Adam, *Modernizing Racial Domination*, Berkeley: University of California Press, 1971. Pierre van den Berghe discusses Afrikaner-English ethnic divisions among South African Whites in his *South Africa: A Study in Conflict*, Berkeley: University of California Press, 1967, Chapter 5.

26. Pierre-Michel Fontaine, "Multinational Corporations and Relations of Race and Color in Brazil," *International Studies Notes*, Vol. 2, Issue 4, Winter, 1975: 8.

27. *Ibid.*, 8.

28. *Ibid.*, 9.

29. A particularly sophisticated study of income maldistribution in Malaysia is: Donald Snodgrass, *Inequality and Economic Development in Malaysia*, unpublished manuscript, mimeo, Harvard University, 1975. Malay attraction to military careers is examined in Enloe, "Civilian Control of the Military: Implications in the Plural Societies of Guyana and Malaysia," in Claude E. Welch, ed., *Civilian Control of the Military*, Albany State University of New York Press, 1976.

30. Fred R. von der Mehden, "Interest Groups and Government Policy in Malaysia," *Rice University Studies*, Vol. 61, No. 4, Fall, 1975: 58. Also see: Von der Mehden, "Communalism, Industrial Policy and Income Distribution in Malaysia," *Asian Survey*, Vol. 15, No. 3, March, 1975: 250-261.

31. Von der Mehden, "Interest Groups and Government Policy in Malaysia," *op.cit.*, 60.

32. K. Das, "Jail, and Tears for Datuk Harun," *Far Eastern Economic Review*, May 28, 1976: 12-13; Andrew Davenport, "Harun, Bad Guy for a Bank," *Far Eastern Economic Review*, May 28, 1976: 99-100.

33. "Northrop: Documenting a Malaysian Connection," *Far Eastern Economic Review*, January 16, 1976: 92-95.

34. Jacques Brazeau and Edouard Cloutier, "Interethnic Relations and the Language Issue in Contemporary Canada: A General Appraisal," Ithaca: Cornell University Center for International Studies, 1975: 16.

35. One of the most useful discussions of the short- and long-term objectives of the New International Economic Order is: Geoffrey Barraclough, "The Haves and Have Nots," *New York Review of Books*, May 13, 1976: 31-41. Goals of the Group of 77 set forth at the UNCTAD 1976 meeting in Nairobi are set forth in Michael T. Kaufman, "U.N. Trade Talks: The Have Nots Demand a Fair Share," *New York Times*, May 17, 1976.

36. Andre Gunder Frank, "Latin America: Underdevelopment or Revolution," Warner Modular Publication, 1973, reprinted from *Monthly Review,* September, 1966. Walter Rodney, *How Europe Underdeveloped Africa,* London: Bogle-L'Ouverture Publications, 1972. Dale L. Johnson, "On Oppressed Classes," in James D. Cockcroft, Andre Gunder Frank and Dale L. Johnson, *Dependence and Underdevelopment,* Garden City, NY: Anchor Books, 1972: 267-301.

37. See Lawrence R. Alschuler, "Satellization and Stagnation in Latin America," *International Studies Quarterly,* Vol. 20, No. 1, March, 1976: 39-82; Christopher Chase-Dunn, "The Effects of International Economic Dependence on Development and Inequality: A Cross-National Study," *American Sociological Review,* Vol. 40, No. 6, December, 1975: 720-738.

38. One study that raises questions about how much effect nationalization of foreign companies have on the status of workers is: John Loxley and John S. Saul, "Multinationals, Workers and Parastatals in Tanzania," *Review of African Political Economy,* No. 2, 1975: 54-88. Ramifications of nationalization of Alcan's bauxite mining operation in Guyana's African-East Indian labor politics is described in Percy C. Hintzen, *Problems of National Integration in Guyana: A Study of Four Urban Areas,* unpublished M.A. Thesis, Clark University, 1975.

GROWTH, MULTINATIONAL CORPORATIONS, AND THE BRAZILIAN STATE

Paul Shankman

Introduction

In the early 1970s, multinational corporate investment proliferated at an unprecedented rate, controlling almost one-third of the Western world's commerce and producing $1 trillion in goods and services annually.[1] The scale of multinational expansion cannot be guaged in sheer dollar terms alone nor can its impact on contemporary economic and political structures be assessed from a strictly national perspective. Increasingly, in corporate circles, there are discussions of the world as a single "integrated unit" and of the necessity for "one world" both politically and economically[2]—a world dominated by multinational corporations. The rationale for this new economic and political order lies in the inadequacies of the nation-state. According to former Undersecretary of State George Ball, the political boundaries of the nation-state are "too narrow to provide adequate scope for modern, large-scale economic activities."[3]

Yet the brave new world of the multinationals has remained a world of nation-states, and despite the alleged obsolescence of the nation-state, there are countries where international firms find their interests best served by the state. In countries such as Brazil, a close relationship between multinational corporations and national government has been mutually beneficial. And if the ultimate question of sovereignty remains unresolved, the collaboration of business and the state has produced an "economic miracle" of sorts.

This paper is concerned with the political and economic arrangements between international firms and the Brazilian state that have produced the "economic miracle," and with the economic, social, and political consequences of these arrangements. Economic growth has been the cornerstone of the partnership between business and the state, and the special type of growth that has occurred in Brazil has both its strengths and limitations. The Brazilian pattern of growth is heavily dependent on a capital-intensive, export-oriented strategy of development, financed in large measure by foreign capital, and geared to the external needs of the world market. While this strategy is sometimes referred to as the "Brazilian model," it is hardly unique to Brazil; the processes taking place in Brazil are occurring throughout the underdeveloped world. Nevertheless, Brazil's sheer size, its geopolitical significance, and the attention given to its economic performance make it a pivotal case for understanding the consequences of a business-state partnership on the economy, social fabric, and political life of a country.

33

In this paper, we shall first examine the role of multinational corporations in Brazil from a national economic perspective, moving from there to analysis of their relationship to inequality, poverty, and deprivation among the Brazilian population. Finally, we shall consider the political consequences of the "Brazilian model," including some recent changes in the partnership of the multinational corporations and the state.

Growth, Multinational Corporations, and the National Economy

Brazil's heralded economic "miracle" began shortly after the military coup of 1964. Since the establishment of the dictatorship, there has been a very strong commitment to economic growth through private foreign investment as well as through state-owned businesses. The policy favoring growth through multinational investment has produced spectacular growth rates—9% to 11% between 1968 and 1974.[4] These growth rates signal the transformation of a previously stagnant economy into an economy with the highest rate of industrialization in Latin America. Manufactured exports increased in value from $109 million in 1965 to $424 million by 1971.[5]

The importance of the multinationals in contributing to the growth of Brazil's economy is considerable. Almost one-half of Brazilian industry is now under multinational control, with American, Japanese, and German firms among the leading foreign investors.[6] The largest global corporations in Brazil include Volkswagen, British-American Tobacco, Ford, Esso, Union Carbide, General Motors, General Electric, Johnson and Johnson, Shell, and Daimler-Benz. Of the 50 largest business enterprises, 42 are either foreign-owned or state-owned; only 8 are owned by Brazilian nationals. These top 50 enterprises receive one-half of the gross profits of the top 500 enterprises in the country.[7] The concentration of profits, especially among the multinationals, reflects the favorable investment climate created and maintained by the military government.

The most profitable and dynamic sectors of the Brazilian economy are dominated by multinational firms. Electrical and non-electrical machinery, chemicals, transportation, rubber, and mining are all controlled by foreign corporations. Although this control existed prior to 1964, it has been intensified during the past decade. In some cases control is virtually complete, as in automobile production (100%), pharmaceuticals (94%), and tobacco (91%).[8] Such control is aided by multinational influence in advertising and in the media. Much of the Brazilian advertising business is in the hands of foreign firms using sophisticated sales techniques. When the largest cigarette manufacturer in Brazil (a company 70% U.S.-British owned) attempts to increase its share of the tobacco market, it employs television advertising methods recently banned in the United States.[9]

34

To reinforce their economic position, multinational firms use a certain amount of social and political leverage to influence Brazilian governmental policies. U.S. businessmen have helped to organize local and American business interests through the creation of the Businessmen's Council Brazil-U.S., a nominally bipartisan group that is now the chief spokesman for the entire private sector. Despite such influence, the multinationals do not always achieve their objectives and may be subject to restrictions such as the Patent Laws of 1970. Nevertheless, the relationship between the multinationals and the military dictatorship has been one of interdependence. As Peter Evans comments:

> Economically, the symbiosis of the military and the multinationals is elegant. It is characterized by a combination of specialization and integrating ties. The state provides entrepreneurship in the public sector and discipline among those who participate in the private sector. But it does not encroach on areas of profitable private investment and they do not threaten the principle of private enterprise on a cultural or ideological level. International firms provide the kind of capital and know-how necessary in the military's ambitions for national prestige and a modern economy. In return, the international firm enjoys a privileged and profitable place in the Brazilian economy.[10]

This close relationship between the military and the global corporations keeps open the vital lines of private foreign capital, international credit, and military aid necessary for political stability and satisfactory profits.

The mutually beneficial relationship between the Brazilian government and private foreign interests, reflected in healthy growth rates, would seem to indicate that the national economy is accumulating capital, and at least in economic terms, is in sound shape. This, however, is *not* the case. Brazil has an adverse trade balance and a soaring foreign debt. While conventional economic wisdom suggests that multinational investment, by generating exports, should reduce trade deficits and the foreign debt, a minority report from the Brazilian Chamber of Deputies challenges this assumption. Noting that multinationals within Brazil may seek foreign sources of credit, the report views such borrowing as a direct cause of foreign debt.

> This [practice] permits a foreign company such as General Motors whose investment is $38 million and reinvestment $45 million, to build up with outside creditors by June of this year [1975] a debt of $200 million, more than 1% of all foreign debt of Brazil.[11]

More significantly, the report found that even when local sources of credit were used, as they commonly are, the export and domestic earnings of the corporations were not providing capital for the development of the national economy. Rather, the multinationals were *decapitalizing* the Brazilian economy through the repatriation of profits and payments for technology. By these means, Johnson and Johnson has taken out 32 times the amount of money it invested in Brazil, while Esso has taken out nearly 25 times the capital it invested. An analysis of 11 multinationals in the minority report revealed that:

> Without a single exception, these firms have remitted in profits and payments for technology more than they have brought here in the form of investments. It is easy to conclude that, contrary to the official argument, the multinationals have brought about a decapitalization of the national economy.[12]

Some of these firms had been in Brazil for as long as 50 years.

Perhaps the most interesting finding of the minority report of the Brazilian Chamber of Deputies is that the military government itself did not have the information necessary to properly assess the consequences of private foreign investment at the national economic level. Beyond crude growth rates, the government had few means of evaluating the actual impact of the multinationals. Lacking the information necessary to formulate sound economic policy, it is not surprising that during the recession of 1974-1975, new economic policies were dictated to a large extent by foreign corporations and international creditors. In order to offset Brazil's trade deficit and to reduce foreign debt, the Brazilian Minister of Finance reoriented the economy to further emphasize exports as well as to reduce and substitute imports. One visible result of this intensification of earlier policy was to drive the nation more deeply into debt. At the same time, slowing growth rates caused worry among creditors about Brazil's ability to service its foreign debt. The *New York Times* reported in its International Economic Survey that the situation had hardly improved by 1978:

> Inflation, which had been as high as 46%, was cut to 38.8% last year (1977) through trimmed Government spending and tight control of money, credit, prices and wages. Gasoline sales were stopped on Sundays. But investment fell, industry expanded at a rate lower than the 2.9 percent annual growth rate of the population, and credit was so restricted that national private businesses feared they were slowly losing out to state-run and multinational companies.[13]

Once again, Brazilian planners turned to exports to provide foreign exchange for oil imports and the servicing of a $30 billion debt.

Viewed from a national economic perspective, the consequences of private foreign investment in Brazil are less positive than they first seemed. Impressive growth rates between 1964 and 1974 cannot be considered in isolation from other national economic trends including equally impressive trade deficits, a heavy foreign debt, and the recent lack of growth. What is more, the ''Brazilian model'' of development may require continued foreign assistance to ''remedy'' the situation. In addition, the emphasis on growth rates as the singular index of modernization has provided the appearance of development while neglecting the problems of inequality, poverty, and deprivation that are also related to multinational investment and to which we shall now turn.

Inequality, Poverty, and Deprivation

While the corporations and Brazilian elite have done quite well by the "miracle," levels of inequality and deprivation have been accentuated. What has happened to the majority of the people under conditions of economic growth is nicely summarized by former President Medici who stated that "the economy is doing well, the people not so well."[14] Indeed, Brazil, with the highest degree of industrialization in Latin America, has the lowest industrial wage rates. And with the highest degree of profitability in South America, Brazil has the highest degree of inequality.[15]

The explicit policy of the government has been to concentrate income in order to promote growth. The concentration of profits is mirrored in the increasingly lopsided income structure of the nation. In an oft-cited study, Robert McNamara of the World Bank notes:

> . . . the share of the national income received by the poorest 40% of the population declined from 10% in 1960 to 8% in 1970, while the share of the richest 5% grew from 29% to 38%.[16]

The wealthiest 5% may actually receive closer to 40% according to Evans and possibly even 50% according to a U.N. study.[17] The distribution of national income is so imbalanced that, despite growth, much of the population has experienced increasing poverty and deprivation.

A number of studies have discussed the declining standard of living for Brazil's masses. Real wage levels have dropped to those existing in the 1950s and they continue to decline in relation to actual purchasing power. In 1965, it was necessary for a blue collar worker in São Paulo to work 87 hours and 20 minutes each month to supply his family with the minimum income for basic food supplies. By 1975, almost twice as much time—176 hours and 54 minutes—was required by the same worker.[18] According to one trade union report, food costs alone could account for 95% of the minimum wage for a worker with a wife and two children; only 5% would remain for housing, clothing, medical care, and other expenses.[19] Such statistics imply a family must have more than one wage earner simply to meet minimal standards, and multiple employment within the family is common. Income, however, remains low because women and children receive lower wages than men. To further complicate matters, the official rate of inflation for 1975 was 31%[20] and in 1976 approached 50%. Even the large wage increases that were put into effect did not offset the spiraling cost of living. For the masses of unemployed, the declining standard of living is even more pressing as social services provided for those out of work are inadequate.

The work force has little protection since the position of organized labor has been eroded by government policies, and union activities are discouraged. As a result, people find compulsory overtime without additional compensation the norm in many industries.[21] Companies may petition the government for additional work scheduling on Sunday and holidays. Although these extensions of the work schedule are supposed to create more jobs, companies frequently compel their regular labor force to work additional days.[22] Job security is lacking, especially in the unskilled and semiskilled occupational categories, and rotation of the labor force through periodic layoffs is a frequent practice.[23]

In urban areas, poverty is intensifying, but more than that, levels of *deprivation* are increasing. That is, conditions are so severe as to jeopardize health and well-being. The work place itself is a major health threat since the lack of safety precautions has allowed Brazil's industrial accident rate to become one of the highest of the world. Low estimates for annual industrial accidents are on the order of 20% of the work force with rates in some industries, such as construction, running over 33% a year.[24] In Brazil's premier industrial metropolis of São Paulo, there are additional health problems. Infant mortality has increased over the past decade, while more recently there have been epidemics of meningitis.[25] A government study found that a majority of São Paulo's population was suffering from malnutrition;[26] this is at a time when multinational advertising was introducing a new consumer product—TV dinners. More generally, an official government report announced that in 1975 the booming region around São Paulo at the very heart of the economic "miracle" had become, along with the semiarid Northeast, the most depressed area in the country. "Indeed," states the report, "urban poverty and its attendant ills have for the first time matched those of the rural areas."[27]

If this is what is happening at the heart of the "miracle," what is occurring on the periphery? It seems that the rural areas are also faring poorly, even in areas where rapid industrialization is taking place. Between 1968 and 1972, the Northeast, long the country's most impoverished area, grew more quickly than the industrial cities of the south. Factories attracted by tax incentives and cheap labor employed about 900,000 workers by 1972. Yet the *Wall Street Journal* found that real income for the workers had not increased and had probably decreased.[28] Furthermore, rural labor has been displaced by mechanization of sugar mills and agriculture.[29] The introduction of cash crops like sisal on subsistence plots has also had an adverse effect, increasing malnutrition and undermining domestic production.[30] Sisal may also displace laborers who then must seek employment either elsewhere in the Northeast or in the troubled industrial cities of the south.[31]

The Amazon is another peripheral area whose vast resources are just being opened by the government and international consortiums.[32] Since parts of this region are still occupied by Indians, a campaign has been launched to eliminate this "barrier" to economic development. The death of the Indians usually follows immediately in the path of progress, through the inadvertant introduction of common diseases and through dislocation caused by road construction.[33] Recently, rich uranium deposits have been discovered on lands used by the well-known Yanomamö Indians. Without protection from disease and dislocation, their fate may have already been sealed.[34]

Economic Distortion

While a thorough explanation of the immiseration of large segments of the Brazilian population is beyond the scope of this paper and would involve many factors other than multinational corporations, recent manifestations of inequality, poverty, and deprivation have been linked to the presence of private foreign investment. In fact, given a policy favoring multinational investment, the discouraging situation in Brazil is hardly unexpected. As economist Albert Fishlow of the University of California at Berkeley comments:

> A market system oriented toward maximum growth, and unencumbered by popular wishes, will almost inevitably emphasize profits at the expense of wages; will almost inevitably tolerate monopoly gains and prevent labor from organizing; will almost inevitably subsidize and attract foreign capital to exploit especially favorable opportunities; will almost inevitably remain open to foreign capital inflows determined by international conditions of supply rather than internal requirements.[35]

In such circumstances, public welfare is likely to be neglected, domestic needs disregarded, and public funds drawn away from the public purpose. As the minority report of the Brazilian Chamber of Deputies notes, multinational operations have not corrected but rather have accentuated distortions in the economic structure, concentrating income in the upper classes and creating consumer demand for luxury items such as color television and large cars, while at the same time undermining the basis for dealing with more pressing social priorities.

An example of this distortion can be found in the shoe manufacturing center of the south where laborers produce footwear, largely for export. Their own shoes are frequently of the second-hand variety donated by American, Canadian, and European charities. The children of these shoe assemblers often have no shoes at all, although this is hardly by choice. The climate and urban environment make shoes a necessity and yet the shoe workers cannot afford to purchase the shoes they produce for themselves or their children. In 1971, production of men's shoes actually decreased due to a domestic "lack of demand."[36]

A second example of economic distortion comes from the Brazilian drug industry, dominated by the multinationals. Although one means of improving health in Brazil would be to provide people with the necessary medicines to combat disease, most basic medicines are priced beyond the reach of the masses. In fact, they are usually priced at levels several times those charged in Europe and the United States despite lower production costs in Brazil. In response to the exorbitant costs of medicine, a nationalist faction within the Brazilian military government requested that they establish an agency to provide drugs at more reasonable rates. As a result, CEME (Central de Medicamentos) was formed in 1971 and the new agency began producing and distributing medicines outside multinational channels. Initially, CEME was successful, but the agency's independence and the competition it provided for the multinationals caused friction. The Director of Cyanamid's Brazilian subsidiary stated:

> CEME should limit itself to the task of producing drugs that private industry initiative is not yet producing. . . . We all agree with the principle that the government must only interfere in the production of goods which private industry cannot produce or has no interest in producing.[37]

In 1975, CEME's position was undermined by a new law weakening the agency's role in research, production, and distribution. The multinationals were thus able to preserve their domination of the national drug market.

A third example of distortion comes from the food industry, 37% of which is under multinational control.[38] If progress is to be made in combating malnutrition and the widespread deficiencies in the Brazilian diet, assistance from international firms will be vital. Yet there has been little effort by the multinationals to help alleviate such deficiencies. Vitamin C is a common deficiency among the population. Interestingly, Brazil produces a large orange crop that could be used domestically to remedy this situation. But most of the orange crop is exported. While nutritious foods are being exported, multimillion dollar advertising campaigns by international firms exhort Brazilian youth to consume soft drinks such as Coca-Cola and Pepsi, as well as Fanta Orange, a Coca-Cola marketed drink without any real orange juice in it. When the nutritional value of these drinks is questioned, corporate spokesmen point to the "psychological" value obtained from their consumption. Indeed, multinational advertising is eager to create psychological value by adapting the product to the local market. In Brazil, the "Pepsi Generation"

40

has become the "Pepsi Revolution." A Brazilian executive in charge of the Pepsi account explains the shift:

> In this country the youth don't have protest channels; the present generation didn't receive any political or social education. So we provide them with a mechanism for protest. It is protest through consumption; the teenager changes from the old-fashioned Coca-Cola and adopts Pepsi, the Pepsi with the young and new image, and he is happy because he is young and young people drink Pepsi.[39]

While the success of diverting political consciousness to status consciousness among an impoverished population remains uncertain, Pepsi has increased its sales with this campaign.

Development, Profit, and "Social Justice"

This brief survey of the economic and social consequences of the Brazilian "miracle" barely scratches the surface. Yet it does indicate that growth in Brazil is occurring in those sectors that are most profitable rather than those most in need of development. With multinational investment given relatively free reign, the pattern of development is uneven, the benefits concentrated, and the transformation of the economy thereby made all the more difficult. A cogent explanation for this paradoxical relationship between profitability and the absence of economic transformation is offered by multinational proponent Harry G. Johnson of the University of Chicago, who notes:

> The corporation's concern in establishing branch operations in a particular developing economy is not to promote development according to any political conception of what development is, but to make satisfactory profits for its management and stockholders. . . . It has no commercial interest in diffusing its knowledge to potential local competitors nor has it any interest in investing more than it has to in acquiring knowlege of local conditions and investigating ways of adapting its own productive knowledge to local factor-price ratios and market conditions. Its purpose is not to transform the economy by exploiting its potentialities—especially its human potentialities—for development, but to exploit the existing situations for its own profit.[40]

Johnson is an advocate, not a critic, of multinational investment, and his analysis differs from other corporate views of recent multinational activity in that it contains no apologetics or rhetoric about social responsibility. Johnson emphasizes that multinational business is no different in its essentials than any other business. Profits are necessary, while social needs and development are not priority items. Johnson has found that multinationals thrive in a general environment of low income and heavy unemployment. Their direct and visible impact is the creation of a small number of jobs, both skilled and unskilled, but beyond a limited number of jobs the beneficial effects of a multinational investment depend on the "exemplary value" of international

41

companies for local enterprises and the use of corporate taxes for education. Johnson warns against incorporating ideas about "social justice" into the investment process, dismissing economic transformations involving more equitable income distribution, adequate wages, and unionization as being "naive" and grounded on "economically debatable assumptions." The net effect of such "well-intentioned measures" would be to hinder multinational investment and corporate profit.

If measures taken to procure social justice are "well-intentioned" but misguided according to multinational proponents, then what of measures taken to insure profitability? Consider the following case.[41] In October 1975, two workers at Coca-Cola's Bonsuccesso (Brazil) plant drowned in a tank of syrup from which 10,000 liters of soda were made before the bodies could be recovered. The company, however, denied allegations of the event, calling accusations by its own workers the fabrications of its rival, Pepsi-Cola. One Coca-Cola official told journalists: "Coca-Cola will give a present to the person who finds the black [worker] who fell into our tank in one of our bottles." Investigations by the Brazilian government into the matter met with little success. Efforts to obtain hospital information and interment certificates were fruitless and no exhumations of the workers' bodies were ordered. Of the three Coca-Cola workers who volunteered to testify, only one gave even preliminary testimony. The second witness was arrested and jailed for "alcoholism," while the third was found dead in a ditch, his fingers and toes burnt off with acid. The official heading the inquiry, on declaring the case closed, said: "Nothing happened; all the workers at the Bonsuccesso plant can turn up dead and I will not take any notice." Subsequently, the Brazilian journalist whose reports uncovered the scandal received anonymous death threats and Coca-Cola threatened to sue him for damaging the company's reputation.

What happened at the Bonsuccesso plant is certainly not representative of the normal pattern of multinational operations. Nevertheless, incidents such as this are sometimes equated with corporate measures to insure profitability. Raymond Vernon of the Harvard Business School has attempted to correct this view, remarking that "hegemony, corruption, waste, inequity, and pollution are not the special hallmarks of the multinational form of enterprise."[42] It is true that such practices can exist without multinationals and even despite their best efforts. As Vernon suggests, however, such practices *can* accompany international business and when they do, they increase the *political* costs of multinational ventures. Because it is the state that is expected to provide political stability and a favorable investment climate, it is also the state that is expected to deal with unfavorable political responses to private foreign investment.

Political Responses to the "Miracle"

Among the masses of Brazil, the intensification of poverty and deprivation coupled with the highest degree of inequality in Latin America have not gone unnoticed nor have incidents such as those at the Bonsuccesso plant. The remarkable thing about these trends is that they have not been accompanied by the political problems from below that might be expected in such circumstances. Active opposition to the dictatorship and the multinationals has been effectively minimized, preserving the stable investment climate so necessary for continued international funding. The lack of effective opposition is, of course, linked to the monopoly of force maintained by the dictatorship. Espionage, torture, censorship, and other repressive means have played a prominent role in the maintenance of the status quo, but there have been other, less obvious means used to consolidate and preserve the political and economic order.

Models of political change in underdeveloped areas often assume that dislocation, deprivation, and inequality are preconditions for change, whether it be manifested in nationalistic revolutions, revitalization movements, ethnic antagonisms, or class struggles.[43] While such models are fundamentally sound, they may fail to predict more muted responses in a modern authoritarian context. In the case of Brazil, it is necessary to examine some aspects of the state apparatus to understand the limitations on effective political opposition from below. To begin with, it is important to dispel the notion that the dictatorship, at its inception, was unpopular and undesirable.

The seizure of power by the Brazilian military in 1964 represented not only the repression of certain political elements and ideologies but also the accommodation of other groups, particularly the upper and upper-middle classes. In his perceptive analysis, political scientist Philippe Schmitter found that the dictatorship installed itself in a "restorationist" rather than in a counter-revolutionary context.[44] By doing so, and without radically transforming the facade of government, the military was able to more easily legitimize its rule and institutionalize its power with a minimum of opposition.

> Under these conditions, one would not anticipate strong resistance from the bourgeois and middle-sector groups steeped in the traditions of political liberalism and angered at having "lost" something that they never had: autonomous participation or hegemony over the political order. Nor would one expect working-class organizations seriously to challenge authority groups with militant demands for greater equality of access or socialization of the means of production. Instead they will be preoccupied with retaining what has already been "benevolently" granted them from above.[45]

Thus a pattern of tacit acceptance of, if not active cooperation with, the dictatorship emerged from a variety of politically pivotal groups: the propertied class, salaried white-collar workers, and the privileged urban working class, who were now somewhat shielded by minimal social legislation from the impoverished masses.

In addition to the cooperation of pivotal groups, the dictatorship has made itself increasingly independent from popular pressure through preemptive means including the penetration of almost all political and economic organizations. For example, the executive branch has sought to mobilize the lowest levels of government—the county and municipal levels—while demobilizing potentially dangerous groups such as organized labor. In the rural areas, after closing down almost all of the rural syndicates and peasant leagues, the government reorganized and extended representation to the rural sector, sponsoring and subsidizing new groups. Throughout the Brazilian polity, critical segments have found themselves incorporated into a single, centrally-coordinated apparatus. Even the other legally-constituted political party finds itself playing by the rules of the dictatorship.

To be certain, there is much more to the twin policies of mobilization and demobilization pursued by the military regime, including ideological indoctrination into the ideas of nationalism and economic growth. The net effect of all these measures has been to make active opposition to the dictatorship extremely difficult. The common bases for political response have been both undermined and rechanneled so that ethnicity, regionalism, and class have failed to catalyze active opposition. Ethnicity has not provided a viable organizational base due to Brazil's complex racial mix. Regionalism, although a factor in the past, has also failed to serve as catalyst, while class relations remain problematic. So carefully has the political arena been circumscribed that only the Catholic Church has expressed its opposition in a coherent manner.

This is not to say that there has been no opposition to the dictatorship and the multinationals. Indeed, the popularity of the opposition party in the 1976 elections clearly demonstrates that even the careful orchestration of authoritarian rule will not always be reflected at the polls. Nevertheless, elections have not significantly altered the policies of the dictatorship. So far the military government seems to have been able to deal with political rivals from below. However, the dictatorship *has* been forced to reconsider its policies due to the changing international economic environment.

In the past, the military regime has closely linked its legitimacy to the rapid growth rates provided by the multinationals. But since the energy crisis of

1973, soaring oil costs have cut severely into the "miracle" and have led the dictatorship to reappraise its reliance on private foreign investment.[46] The rising foreign debt, the rising trade deficits, and the inevitable crunch on the masses have not merely cost the government popular support. The recession has caused it to reexamine the effects of multinationals on the national economy. When the economy was booming, the partnership of state and foreign business was mutually advantageous, but during times of economic difficulty, the economic and even the political role of the multinationals is being questioned. Recent government studies show the negative effect of multinationals on the balance of trade and foreign debt, and segments of the government have chosen to blame the multinationals for Brazil's economic problems. In 1976, the *Wall Street Journal* described letters of reprimand sent out to scores of foreign companies by the Brazilian government followed up by official face-to-face confrontations with corporate executives.[47] Since multinationals have been accustomed to a friendly working relationship with the military regime, their new role as scapegoat has come as something of a shock. Moreover, foreign businesses are concerned that their position may be jeopardized by new economic policies subordinating multinational interests to those of the state.

The economic policies currently pursued by the dictatorship emphasize state-owned corporations and import substitution. State capitalism seems to be the wave of the future. Yet these new directions are not without their difficulties. Since its inception, international contacts and support have been carefully nurtured by the Brazilian military. The response by both public and private agencies abroad has been generous, but it is based on a certain *quid pro quo*. Just as new economic policies encroach on private foreign investment, so they threaten the international support for a regime that has been so important. As Schmitter observes:

> Should foreign capitalists, international civil servants, or United States officials lose confidence in the Brazilian military's capacity to guarantee stability, or conversely, should these outsiders decide that long-term authoritarian rule will not protect their economic or political interests, the system could be in trouble.[48]

While this scenario seems unlikely, the relationship between the multinationals and the state has taken on an adversary quality. One corporate manager describes the situation in the business realm as follows:

> We are playing with them. . . . They gave us an edict telling us to cut imports of components and start producing them in Brazil. We told them we can't, at least not for a long time. They came back that we must. We then asked them if they wanted us to shut down—that's what will happen if they don't loosen up. The next move is theirs. This'll go on until we reach a compromise.[49]

45

Conclusion

Only a few years ago the alliance between the multinational corporations and the Brazilian state seemed so secure that few analysts could have foreseen the rifts that have, in fact, emerged. In retrospect it is evident that these rifts were present, although submerged, during the period of economic growth. As growth slackened and as costs of this type of growth fell more heavily on the government, the rifts began to surface. Thus the relationship between the multinationals and the state seems constrained by the very process of growth that made the alliance workable in the first place.

In the past, multinational investment in Brazil was easily equated with growth and development by both international firms and the state. It is apparent, though, that this is more an ideology than a reality. Certainly the consequences of the partnership between foreign businesses and the state cannot be encompassed entirely by the terms growth and development. Yet the ideology of growth through private foreign investment persists. Recently, IBM Chairman Jacques Maisonrouge commented that:

> . . .despite the increasing suspicion and criticism that the "cult" of growth has been subjected to recently, it still represents our best hope for the future, not because growth by and of itself is desirable, but because many of its byproducts are. Among those byproducts are the creation of new jobs, new wealth, and higher living standards, which in turn result in closing the various gaps—economic, educational, and technological— that have always fueled human jealousy, hatred, and conflicts.[50]

Unfortunately, for most of the Brazilian people the desirable "byproducts" of growth through multinational investment have not materialized. In many cases, multinationals have eliminated jobs, while new employment opportunities have not created new wealth or higher living standards for the majority of the population. Some of the direct and measurable "byproducts" of growth in Brazil are a national economy in trouble, and the intensification of inequality, poverty, and deprivation; these are characteristics usually associated with underdevelopment rather than with development.

The few benefits that have materialized have accrued primarily to the corporations and the top 20% of the population. Thus, far from "closing the gaps" in Brazilian society, the consequences of multinational investment have tended to widen them, making the military dictatorship an essential ingredient in the preservation of the economic status quo. Yet during the period of low growth, the costs of maintaining the status quo have risen to the point where the government is apparently dissatisfied with its acquiescence to foreign economic interests and the multinational corporations have found themselves under fire. The military regime itself has experienced criticism,

46

including a questioning of the notion that authoritarian rule is a prerequisite for economic growth. Antonio Pimenta Neves of the *Gazeta Mercantil* of São Paulo has articulated this position recently, stating:

> The claim that authoritarian regimes are essential to economic and social development is demonstrably false. Brazil experienced as much growth under Juscelino Kubitschek as it has after the 1964 military coup—and we experienced it with freedom. Thirteen years later we are in very much the economic situation that preceded the coup—without freedom. We again are suffering from rampant inflation and political instability. Another point was that corruption was suppressed. Yet in recent years Brazil has experienced more corruption than under the regime of constitutional freedom, and it is corruption of the worst kind—many of the corruptors are never known and many corruptions are covered up.[51]

The situation has become troublesome for all parties concerned.

If recent events in Brazil have highlighted the potentially antagonistic relationship between multinational corporations and the state, it would seem that a return to a period of rapid growth might improve that relationship. Such a period of growth notwithstanding, the tensions that have surfaced are unlikely to vanish entirely. The persistence of these tensions can be explained in terms of an inherent conflict between two fundamentally different modes of organizing economic life—a vertical mode finding its expression in centrally organized, transnational corporate structures of production, and a horizontal mode expressed in the jealously-guarded prerogatives of the nation-state.[52] Robert Heilbroner has found that, regardless of whether corporations or the state dominate in a particular instance, the conflict remains. He concludes that while multinational expansion has posed new problems and challenges for both the economic production mechanism and the political control mechanism in underdeveloped countries, corporations do not currently provide an alternative to the nation-state or pose a threat to it.[53] For its part, the state—in countries like Brazil—cannot easily extricate itself from the web of economic ties and the pattern of growth it has found itself committed to. And so, the uneasy relationship between multinationals and the Brazilian state is likely to continue, with fluctuations in growth rates tempering or heightening problems, but never truly resolving them.

FOOTNOTES

1. R. Barnet and R. Müller present a vast array of data on multinational expansion in their book *Global Reach: The Power of Multinational Corporations* (New York: Simon and Schuster, 1974). While this paper reflects some of the interpretations in *Global Reach,* this author's point of view is more fully developed in "Notes on a Corporate 'Potlatch' " (Paul Shankman in *The World as a Company Town,* E. and A. Idris-Soven and M. Vaughn, eds., World Anthropology Series, The Hague: Mouton, in press).

2. H.G. Johnson, "The Multinational Corporation as a Development Agent," *Columbia Journal of World Business* 5 (1970): 25-30.

3. G. Ball, "Introduction," *Global Companies: The Political Economy of World Business,* G. Ball, ed., Englewood Cliffs (New Jersey): Prentice-Hall, 1975.

4. B. Handler, "Flying Down to Rio," *New York Times* Magazine Section, June 8, 1975: 16. For a detailed analysis of growth during this period, see E. Bacha, "Issues and Evidence on Recent Brazilian Economic Growth," *World Development* 5 (1977): 46-67.

5. Barnet and Müller, *Global Reach,* 128.

6. R. Newfarmer and W. Mueller, "Multinational Corporations in Brazil and Mexico: Structural Sources of Economic and Noneconomic Power," in *Report to the Subcommittee on Multinational Corporations of the Committee on Foreign Relations,* Washington, D.C.: Government Printing Office, 1975: 106-107.

7. *Ibid.,* 106.

8. *Ibid.,* 111.

9. Barnet and Müller, *Global Reach,* 144.

10. P.B. Evans, "The Military, the Multinationals, and the 'Miracle': the Political Economy of the 'Brazilian Model' of Development," *Studies in Comparative International Development* 9 (1974): 26-45.

11. *Los Angeles Times* (part 3), December 1, 1975: 14.

12. *Ibid.*

13. *New York Times* International Economic Survey, February 5, 1978: 90.

14. H.B. Burns, "Brazil: the Imitative Society," *Nation* 215 (1972): 17-20.

15. Evans, "The Military, the Multinationals. . . ," 35.

16. R. McNamara "Development in the Developing World: The Maldistribution of Income," *Vital Speeches of the Day* 38 (1972): 482-487.

17. Cited in Barnet and Müller, *Global Reach,* 150.

18. Handler, "Flying Down to Rio," 89.

19. "Living on the Minimum," *Brazilian Information Bulletin* no. 17 (1975): 13.

20. *Business Week.* August 9, 1976: 34.

21. H. de Souza, "The Multinationals and the Exploitation of the Working Class in Brazil," in *The Multinational Corporations and Brazil,* M. Arruda, et al., eds., Brazilian Studies Latin America Research Unit, 1975: 15.

22. *Ibid.,* 16.

23. *Ibid.,* 14.

24. *Ibid.,* 18.

25. *New York Times* (part 3), June 22, 1975: 3.

26. *Ibid.*

27. *Ibid.,* January 25, 1976: 3.

28. *Wall street Journal,* April 14, 1972, p. 1, and April 21, 1972: 1.

29. *Barnet and Müller, Global Reach,* 169-170.

30. D. Gross and B. Underwood, "Technological Change and Caloric Costs: Sisal Agriculture in Northeastern Brazil," *American Anthropologist* 73 (1971): 725-740.

31. For a description of the life of northeastern migrants in Brazilia, see D. Epstein, *Brazilia: Plan and Reality* (Berkeley: University of California Press, 1973).

32. "Brazil: Let Them Eat Minerals," *NACLA's Latin America and Empire Report* 7 (1973): 3-13.

33. For a description of this process see Shelton Davis, *Victims of the "Miracle": Development Against the Indians of Brazil* (New York: Cambridge University Press, 1977). In this volume, Davis carefully analyzes the role of the Brazilian government and the multinational corporations in the destruction of the Indians.

34. "Uranium Discovery Threatens Tribe," *Brazilian Information Bulletin* 17 (1975): 6-10.

35. "The Weight of the Wealthy," *ibid.,* 14 (1974): 8.

36. M. Arruda, "Notes on the Situation of Labour in Contemporary Brazil," in *The Multinational Corporations and Brazil,* M. Arruda et al., eds., Brazilian Studies Latin America Research Unit, 1975: 44.

37. Cited in R.J. Ledogar, *Hungry for Profits: U.S. Food and Drug Multinationals in Latin America* (IDOC/North America no. 70, 1975): 69. The entire book is informative.

38. This example is also taken from Ledogar (*ibid.*, 111-126).

39. Cited in Ledogar (*ibid.*).

40. Johnson, "The Multinational Corporation as a Development Agent," 26.

41. *Colorado Daily,* August 27, 1976: 9.

42. R. Vernon, "Storm Over the Multinationals: Problems and Prospects," *Foreign Affairs* 55 (1977): 43-62.

43. E. Wolf, *Peasant Wars of the 20th Century.* New York: Harper & Row, 1969. M. Hechter, *Internal Colonialism: The Celtic Fringe in British National Development, 1536-1966.* Berkeley, University of California Press, 1975.

44. P. Schmitter, "The 'Portugalization' of Brazil," in *Authoritarian Brazil,* New Haven: Yale University Press, 1973: 186.

45. *Ibid.*

46. See "Brazil Dreams of Glory—And the Rude Awakening," *U.S. News and World Report,* October 18, 1976: 91-94; and "Brazil Puts the Head on Foreign Firms as Boom Cools Down," *Wall Street Journal,* October 8, 1976: 1, 23.

47. *Wall Street Journal,* October 8, 1976.

48. Schmitter, "The 'Portugalization' of Brazil," 230.

49. *Wall Street Journal,* October 8, 1976, 23.

50. J. Maisonrouge, "How a Multinational Corporation Appears to Its Managers," in *Global Companies: The Political Economy of World Business,* Englewood Cliffs (New Jersey): Prentice-Hall, 1975: 15.

51. *Wall Street Journal,* November 25, 1976: 14.

52. R. Heilbroner, *Business Civilization in Decline,* New York: Norton, 1976: 95-96.

53. *Ibid.,* 95. A similar point is made in P. B. Evan's analysis of the relationship between multinationals and state-owned corporations in Brazil ("Multinationals, State-Owned Corporations, and the Transformation of Imperialism: A Brazilian Case Study," *Economic Development and Cultural Change* 26 (1977): 43-64.)

CARIBBEAN RESPONSES TO THE INTERNATIONAL POLITICAL ECONOMY: EFFORTS TOWARD SYSTEM CHANGE

Pierre-Michel Fontaine
Leslie I. Hill

Introduction

A major characteristic of the Caribbean has been its traditional domination by the Western international politico-economic system. This is where Europe established its earliest full-fledged colonies in modern times, and it may be where Western colonial or semi-colonial appendages will disappear last. One may, therefore, postulate a condition of early colonization/late decolonization as a major determining characteristic of Caribbean political economy.

The most salient historical manifestation of European imperial-capitalist presence has been the plantation structure.[1] The plantation is not merely an economic organization, but is rather a way of life that has dominated, and still strongly influences the economic, political, social, and cultural structures and processes of Caribbean formations.[2] The plantation system was established in an area that had been swiftly emptied of its indigenous inhabitants. Indeed, only Guyana, among the countries that concern us in this paper, possesses a small AmerIndian population. Typically plantations were run by European owners—mostly absentee—and managers, and worked by African slaves, with later substitutions of East Indian, Chinese, and even Portuguese, especially in Trinidad and Guyana.

The economy and the ethnic composition of Caribbean societies was fashioned by Europeans in response to the needs of their international economic system. This was also true, of course, of the social structures and political institutions. These societies did not remain static. As they evolved roughly from the slave plantation through the indenture plantation and the corporate plantation to the metropolitan plantation enterprise *cum* multinational corporation, corresponding changes took place in the political regimes and the social systems.[3] Though Trinidad and Tobago, Jamaica, and Guyana have achieved independence, the first two in 1962 and the third in 1966, their basic relationship of dependency *vis-à-vis* Western metropolitan powers has continued. At best, the achievement of "independence" constituted the political equivalent of the ongoing shift of economic dependency ties from Great Britain to the United States.[4]

With respect to Jamaica, it has been argued that a genuine self-determination movement leading to independence was nonexistent and that there was "nothing which can properly be labelled as a nationalist movement."[5] Jamaican nationalism, for the most part, was the nationalism of the so-called new middle class—an incipient, embryonic, or aspiring national bourgeoisie.[6] Independence did mean, however, that within certain limits the middle class could benefit from a broader range of international linkages and thereby accelerate its process of consolidation and expansion. It also meant that the Caribbean masses would become less inclined to see the members of the middle class as fellow victims of colonial oppression but more as accomplices of expatriate economic interests.

The interplay between the tendency of the local elites to consolidate themselves and that of the masses and their leaders and organizations to demand account will determine national responses to the challenges and opportunities offered by the international politico-economic system. In a first stage, with the masses under control, the new rulers may attempt to consolidate their power by reinforcing the extant regime of external economic relations—that is, by increasing their integration into the Western international economic system. In a later phase, when the masses are mobilizing into a political force, selective disengagement may occur, and there will be attempts to renegotiate, to transform, or perhaps to reduce the terms of dependency. In a hypothetical third stage—presumably, in this region, reached only by Cuba—full disengagement from the Western system would be attempted.

The purpose of this paper is to explore the evolution of Caribbean responses to foreign investment, particularly direct investment by multinational corporations. The multinationals are the most dynamic transnational economic actors and salient in the eyes of all social classes and ethnic groups in the Caribbean. They have controlled important economic sectors in these countries—the sugar industry in Trinidad and Tobago, Jamaica, and Guyana, bauxite and alumina in Jamaica and Guyana, and petroleum in Trinidad. Before looking at the interaction between MNCs and Caribbean social formations, it is important to examine the nature of Caribbean political regimes to understand the political economy of the region. In our efforts to apprehend social reality we will attempt to heed Fernando Henrique Cardoso's advice about the virtues of historical-structural analysis.[7]

Political Regimes and Political Economy

Because Caribbean political and economic systems have been penetrated deeply, the notions of "political regime" and "political economy" gain their full meaning only in a transnational perspective. One consequence of the early colonization/late decolonization syndrome in the Commonwealth Caribbean is a high degree of internalization by the middle and upper classes of the values, ideals, and attitudes consistent with the Westminsterian model of government. Commitment to the British-style parliamentary system was especially obvious in Jamaica, where a two-party system had already developed during the period of self-government. Even the Marxist Dr. Jagan in then-British Guiana is said to have evidenced "a definite preference for parliamentary government."[8] Accordingly, we are told that of the "difficult national decisions" faced by the British West Indies in the late 1950s and early 1960s, "the form of government, broadly speaking, was one of the least traumatic transitional issues."[9] Underpinning the parliamentary governmental institutions are functioning party systems. In Jamaica, Guyana, and now Trinidad, two major parties dominate the political arena.

With the exceptions of Dr. Eric Williams and the People's National Congress (PNG), practically all principal leaders and parties in the Commonwealth Caribbean have been associated with thriving, turbulent labor unions which have provided a framework for popular support. Both the superstructure and the infrasturcture of the Westminsterian model have been well established, insofar as those institutions have been the instrument of control of the new elites in the seats of governmental power.

These instruments have been modified in response to the requirements of power consolidation. To stop Marxist, pro-Soviet Dr. Cheddi Jagan and his People's Progressive Party (PPP), the British, at the urging of the United States, introduced proportional representation in British Guyana in October 1963. This favored Forbes Burnham, who became Prime Minister of a coalition government as a result of the 1964 elections. Various accusations of electoral irregularities have been made against Burnham over the years. In Guyana, further modifications were made when the country became a Republic in 1970, eliminating the post of Governor General and substituting a President. In Trinidad and Tobago, recent Constitutional reforms established a republican form of government. Such changes are being contemplated in Jamaica as well. Meanwhile, in all three countries and elsewhere in the Caribbean, there have been various restrictive legislations aimed especially at curbing labor militancy and dissident political activities.

In this political context of modified parliamentarism, major economic decisions were made. It is important to realize the imperial political bases of multinational corporate establishments in the Caribbean. The metropolitan plantation enterprises in the sugar industry, such as Tate & Lyle in Trinidad and Tobago and in Jamaica, and Booker McConnell and Jessell Enterprises in Guyana, were direct historical extensions of the old plantation systems of the colonial period.[10] The multinational firms in the mineral sector, such as

Aluminum of Canada (ALCAN) and Reynolds in bauxite in Guyana and in Jamaica, together with Kaiser, Aluminum Company of America (ALCOA), and later Revere and Alpart, entered these countries primarily during the colonial period under contracts negotiated with colonial governments. The symbiotic relationship between private interests and imperial decision-makers as they affected the Caribbean has been well documented in Guyana.[11] The economic rivalry between United States and British private interests over Guyanese bauxite manifested itself early. The creation of ALCAN by ALCOA was an offshoot of this competition; it allowed ALCOA to circumvent British regulations, setting up a "British" company by virtue of its having the nationality of a dominion—Canada.[12]

In the fields of manufacturing and tourism, also established prior to independence, the U.S. connection manifested itself vigorously. The banking sector, created first to service the plantation, was also controlled by metropolitan interests. Subsequently, U.S. banks began moving into the area, significantly influencing banking practices.

The important decisions concerning the direction of Caribbean economies were not random, but consistent with the continuing, evolving, imperial order. They responded to a certain perception about Caribbean society shared by old and new elites and the metropolitan powers. The model of development prevailing during the transition era (post World War II) has been called, somewhat derisively, "industrialization by invitation." It assumes that while foreign investment is badly needed, it will not come into the area unless lured in by special incentives. At the time, of course, it was generally "assumed that dependence was the natural state of the Caribbean territories."[13]

The paternity of the school of thought which advocated this variant of the Puerto Rican model (Operation Bootstrap) is generally attributed to the West Indian economist W. Arthur Lewis. The argument is predicated on the small size and low income of Caribbean societies, which mean small markets unattractive to the investor.[14] In this situation one solution is to attract foreign investors who produce goods for export, but to do so, they must be guaranteed high profits through incentives, the mainstay of which are tax holidays.[15] Economist G. E. Cumper has contested Norman Girvan's interpretation of W. Arthur Lewis's position, arguing that Lewis's recommendations on foreign investment were merely tactical and in response to the colonial government's opposition to any form of "industrial or financial intervention." Strategically, and even sometimes tactically, Lewis believed strongly that development depended on local savings and that the West Indies did have the required capital.[16]

Industrial development corporations were created in Trinidad and Tobago, in Jamaica, in Guyana, and elsewhere in the region. Industrial incentive laws and export industry encouragement laws were passed area wide in the 1950s, creating a situation of fierce competition and of ever-escalating incentives in the effort to attract foreign investors.[17] A variety of investors, including multinational corporations, participated. Some objectives have been achieved: per capita income, domestic savings and local enterpreneurship have expanded, and there has been considerable industrial and economic growth. However, income redistribution has been minimal and the already serious problem of unemployment has been exacerbated. More importantly, the increase in direct foreign investment has had significant negative effects leading to a crisis in the Caribbean political economy.

Multinational Corporations and Caribbean Political Economy

Aside from generous incentives granted to companies, few guidelines in terms of land use, production levels, or employment of nationals, were adopted.

In examining the terms of company-country agreements in the area, Norman Girvan highlighted company objectives and country concessions. He describes four general areas useful for this discussion. First is resource accessibility, where the objective of the companies is to secure rights to seek and to exploit as much of a given resource as possible, and to secure exclusive rights to natural resources needed in the production process of the resource in order to "maximize and monopolize."[18] The second area is operational conditions. The objective here is to escape the general legislation and administration of the country as much as possible.[19] The third area involves the payment stream to the government. The company's purpose is to reduce the payments, fixing them within narrow limits to stabilize and minimize the payment stream.[20] The fourth area involves the status of the agreement: companies try to maximize the length of agreements and to control the process of change.[21]

Despite the expectation of Caribbean governments that direct foreign investment would provide capital, technology, employment, government revenues and foreign exchange, development of local facilities and local markets, and managerial and organizational skills, the terms of the agreements severely limited their maximization of such benefits. In economic terms, the large initial investment of foreign capital to develop and to generate industrial growth in the Caribbean was substantial. It is assumed that it would be extremely difficult for these underdeveloped countries to raise the large amount of capital needed for initial investment in industry. It is, however, questionable whether direct private foreign investment was the most appropriate form of capital mobilization. Furthermore, it is not uncommon for corporations, once the initial investment has been made, to raise subsequent investment capital out of local savings within the host country. This, of course, further strengthens the dependency relationship.[22]

Another benefit cited frequently in the establishment of multinational corporate investment is the acquisition of technological and managerial skills by the host country. Provisions were often made in company-country agreements for management personnel to be provided by the parent corporation.[23] Seldom were host country citizens employed in such positions. This is strange in countries like Guyana and Surinam where operations have continued for over fifty years. Over the decades, personnel continued to be drawn from "the country, the culture-group and the racial group, from which the ownership and control of the firm is derived."[24] In this way the firm hoped to prevent conflict between its goals, values, and ethos, and those of the host country from interfering with the smooth and profitable functioning of the corporate organization.

Unemployment is a chronic problem in the Caribbean; estimated levels run as high as twenty to twenty-five percent. The annual growth of the labor force exacerbates this problem. It was expected that the labor requirements of the foreign companies would help reduce the high rates of unemployment and absorb some of the growth in the labor supply. In almost all cases this has not been the result. Unemployment levels remain high. In fact, in Trinidad and Tobago, employment in the public sector had increased faster than in the private sector by the late 60s.[25] This failure to absorb a large part of the labor supply is due primarily to the capital-intensive nature of the industrial operations established by the corporations. The petroleum industry in Trinidad and Tobago accounts for thirty percent of the Gross National Product, but employs only five percent of the Trinagoan labor force.[26] In Jamaica, the bauxite industry accounts for ten percent of the Gross Domestic Product and forty-seven percent of domestic exports, but employs only one percent of the Jamaican labor force.[27]

Furthermore, the nondevelopment of peripheral industry limits the employment possibilities of the industrial sector. Where employment of the local labor supply does occur, it exacerbates the chronic problem of income distribution because it further establishes income differentials between industrial workers and the work force employed in less lucrative positions.

Another issue is that of government revenues. The payment stream of corporate operations in the Caribbean contributes significant portions of government revenues through taxes, customs duties, and the like. Even so, because of the nature of the "industrialization by invitation" program with its extensive concessions to corporations, there is a substantial discrepancy between existing and potential revenues from corporate operations, especially in the manufacturing sector.

Another loss of government revenue arises from the integrated nature of firms across national boundaries, especially in the natural resources sector. Because firms usually establish only one level of the production process in a host country, a substantial portion of revenue is lost to metropolitan countries where refining, fabricating, and marketing operations are carried out. Girvan has noted that "in transferring a ton of bauxite into semi-fabricated aluminum the value rises from between W.I. $14 and $28 to somewhere in the region of $350."[28] A similar relationship between stage of production and level of income exists in the agricultural sector, as in the case of sugar in Jamaica.[29]

The infrastructure needed to operate these industries—electricity, roads, and water supply—contributes to national development of the host country. However, the government incurs the construction debt, and the services are sometimes owned by the company and sold to the government and/or citizens.

Other issues affect the political economy: development of local market and local industry, depletion of natural resources, industrial blight, population shifts and urbanization, uneven development of different sectors of the economy, and social, political, and cultural consequences. A serious political cost is the host country's loss of effective control over the exploitation, production, and allocation of its resources, a result of negotiated company-country agreements, MNC structure, and the international market. The vertical integration of the multinational corporation allows it to move goods and capital within the corporation with the least financial liability to governments (taxes, duties). For example, mineral resources and agricultural products exported out of the host country are not usually sold on the open market. They are often "sold" to the mother corporation at less than the market price and, usually, the products are refined, manufactured, or fabricated before being marketed as finished products.

In addition, there are restrictions on the freedom of the government to act on its own behalf in such areas as negotiation with other countries and with transnational organizations for markets for the country's products, and certain internal government operations where economic interests are involved. All of these activities must be carried out by the government with the interests of the multinational corporations and other foreign companies in mind so as not to jeopardize foreign investment. The government must create and maintain a "favorable investment climate."

Corporate executives from metropolitan countries exert control over economic structures and have influence over political decision-making. Certain values are maintained. In some cases, linkages between specific groups are reinforced; in others, distinctions between groups are upheld. Not only are values related to race and class stratification reinforced, but those values linked with the extension of capitalism—profit maximization, competition, and consumerism—are transferred.

Antagonisms, stratifications and racial and ethnic cleavages are integral to the Caribbean political economy. This was true under slavery and continues in the post-independence era.[30] With respect to the multinational corporations, Maurice St. Pierre has shown how racist policies of the Demerara Bauxite Company (Demba), a Guyanese subsidiary of ALCAN, provoked a political struggle on the part of the workers, and created the basis for the later nationalist policies of the People's National Congress (PNC) toward Demba.[31] When the assault on the Caribbean political economy began manifesting itself in the late 60s, its most salient and certainly most widespread manifestation was the so-called Caribbean Black Power Movement.

The Crisis of the Caribbean Political Economy

By the late 60s, industrialization by invitation had failed to solve the problems of the Caribbean, even though it had brought about economic growth and an enlargement and a strengthening of the local entrepreneurial class and government bureaucracy. In fact, social problems appeared to have been aggravated over the period. Unemployment stood at intolerably high levels, and it is not surprising that the unemployed provided much of the membership of the marches and demonstrations of the 1970 Black Power revolt in Trinidad. Meanwhile, after the euphoria of the early years of independence, political stagnation came to prevail in Jamaica, where the Jamaica Labor Party (JLP) dominated the decade of the 60s with the People's National Party (PNP) in the opposition. The same situation existed in Trinidad and Tobago under the PNM. In Guyana, the political situation in the wake of the communal strife of the early 60s was enlivened by active ethnic antagonism between the East Indian-dominated PPP and the African-dominated PNC. In reality, the Caribbean version of the Westminsterian system had been very oppressive toward the masses, both during the colonial period and after independence, as witnessed by the labor riots of the 1930s.

The so-called labor disturbances of the 1930s were the continuation of a long tradition of periodic revolts. They prepared the ground for the emergence

58

of the labor movement and the establishment of political parties in the area. Eventually, the popular anger which they embodied was sublimated into a struggle for self-government. As indicated earlier, while "constitutional decolonization" somewhat increased the options of the new elites, it also exposed them to direct accusations of collusion with imperialism and foreign economic interests.

At the same time, the Caribbean Westminsterian model of government, in spite of its restrictive and coercive features, allowed critical debate and organization around the issues of Caribbean political economy—at least up to the threshold of transformation of talk into mass action. What was not tolerated was a movement of truly popular nature, that of the Rastafarian Brethren. The Rastafaris were of the same forces that led to the riots of the 1930s. By virtue of their total rejection of Afro-Saxon culture, they had not been transformed by the movement toward self-government, and their culture was still intact by the late 60s.[32]

The University of the West Indies (UWI) played a role in these movements, as professors and students provided part of the leadership. The New World Group was set up in 1963 as a forum for discussion of policy issues from a radical perspective. Lloyd Best and James Millette (its chief officer of Trinidad), Miles Fitzpatrick, Steve DeCastro, Archie Singham, and Alister McIntyre of Jamaica, and later Walter Rodney and Clive Y. Thomas of Guyana, played major roles in it. (The Group published *New World Fortnightly* from March 1963 to 1966 and then *New World Quarterly* from 1965 on. The *Quarterly* was a proponent of Caribbean integration.) The New World Group foundered in the wake of the JLP government's refusal in 1968 to allow Walter Rodney, history lecturer at UWI, to reenter Jamaica after participating in a writer's conference in Canada. The Group split under the respective pulls of Lloyd Best, who wanted it to remain "independent" and "objective" in the face of the escalating events, and James Millette, who wanted it to be transformed into an active political party.

Best went on to form Tapia House in Trinidad, whose pamphlets and weekly newspaper *Tapia* have provided sophisticated analyses of the political and economic situation in Trinidad and the Caribbean. Tapia House transformed itself into a political party in 1976.[33] James Millette formed a radical group in Trinidad that became the United National Independence Party (UNIP) in 1969. Millette was part of the leadership that established a working class coalition in 1975 uniting sugar cane workers and farmers with oil and transport workers. During 1976 parliamentary elections, the group adopted a resolution "demanding the withdrawal of multinationals from the country."[34] As late as 1974 **Tapia House** had limited itself to asking for "localization" of foreign firms through joint ventures and local private and government participation.[35] Millette's group, however, was advocating that the entire foreign sector, including oil, be nationalized.[36] This was farther than even C.L.R. James's Workers and Farmers Party (1966) had been willing to go since it excluded the oil industry from its call for nationalization. In 1970 in Trinidad, the internationally-based New Beginning Movement was formed. It publishes the monthly *Caribbean Dialogue* and has produced a series of radical analyses of the Caribbean political economy.[37]

In the late 60s, Trinidad also saw the emergence of Geddes Granger's National Joint Action Committee (NJAC) which spearheaded the so-called February Revolution or Black Power Revolt of 1970. NJAC was opposed to the foreign banks, especially the Canadian banks (presumably because of the Canadian role in triggering these disturbances), to Tate & Lyle's dominance of the sugar industry, and to Texaco's preponderance in oil, though it does not seem to have asked for the latter's nationalization.[38]

Trinidad has seen the births of other radical and anti-establishment organizations. Such were New Day, absorbed into NJAC, the National Union of Freedom Fighters (NUFF), and Errol Balfour's Union of Revolutionary Organizations (URO). The latter has specifically attacked the "industrialization by invitation" model, the developmentalist thesis of the U.N. Economic Commission for Latin America (ECLA), as well as partnership and localization, and has supported socialist planning.[39]

In Jamaica, a Black Power group called Abeng, which had close ties with the Rastas, was forced to disband under pressures from the JLP government. Its publication was also called *Abeng*. In opposition to the establishment Bustamante Industrial Trade Union (JLP affiliate), dominant in the sugar industry, and the National Workers Union (PNP affiliate), dominant in the bauxite and tourist sectors, there arose the Independent Trade Union Action Council (ITAC), which published *Worker's Monthly* and served as an umbrella organization for such radical unions as Professor Trevor Munroe's University and Allied Workers Union (UAWU). Both worked closely with the anti-establishment Union of Democratic Students (UDS).

In Guyana, radical intellectuals at the University formed a discussion group called Ratoon, which published a journal of the same name. Barbadian activists published *Bim* (essentially literary) and *Manjac*. A group called Forum was formed in St. Vincent. And the Grenadian government has had to deal with a Black Power organization called New Jewel Movement, which posed a physical threat to banks and other foreign firms and is now a member of the opposition coalition which emerged in the fall 1976 parliamentary elections. In other words, the late 60s and early 70s proved to be a period of considerable intellectual and popular ferment on the Left in the Commonwealth Caribbean. In this regard, Guyana is different from the rest, as this function on the Left has been largely, though not entirely, performed since the early fifties by the PPP, which is in fact an established political party, the largest in the country. This perhaps explains why nationalization of a Commonwealth Caribbean mining multinational—Demba (ALCAN)—took place first in Guyana. Dr. Jagan was perhaps referring to this when he said, in explaining the PPP's recent policy of "critical support" to the PNC, that the latter "has no principled position. . . its moves are largely determined by countervailing pressures."[40]

It was in the so-called Black Power Movement that the critical mass between intellectual speculation and discussion, on the one hand, and popular action on the other was achieved. The legacy of the plantation is such that in those predominantly black societies, racial and ethnic stratification still prevails, albeit in modified fashion. It is not only that such people are generally poor and victims of discrimination or that upper echelons in multinationals and other foreign firms tend to be occupied by white expatriates;[41] more importantly it was widely agreed that political leaders, because of their colonial and racial mentality, had no confidence in their people or even in themselves.[42]

In approaching the problems of dependency and neo-colonialism, the movement attempted to identify the role of national governments and elites as instruments of dependency. Of late, that local ruling elite has incorporated a number of blacks in positions of prominence. However, regardless of its racial or color composition, this power-group is merely representing metropolitan-imperialist interests. This elite is simply an agent of the whites in the metropolis, with an army and a police force designed to maintain the imperialist way.[43]

The first uprising occurred in Jamaica in October 1968 and began as a nonviolent protest of University students against the government's ban on Dr. Walter Rodney. It was joined by citizens, and the police eventually attacked the marchers. In the ensuing escalation, three demonstrators were killed, a number of fires were started, several buses were burned, and some persons identified as "enemies of the people" were spat upon and beaten. The Student-Staff Action Committee noted that the targets of attack were the Royal Bank of Canada, the Bank of London and Montreal, North American Life, and Woolworth.[44]

A similar uprising took place in Trinidad in February 1970. Students from the University of the West Indies led a demonstration in Port-of-Spain to protest the trial of West Indian students in Canada charged with the destruction of a computer center at Sir George Williams University in Montreal. Several hundred marched to the Canadian High Commission, the Royal Bank of Canada, and the Roman Catholic Cathedral. In the following weeks several demonstrations and marches occurred, and there were police attacks and arrests of political and labor leaders under a State of Emergency. At this time U.S. and Venezuelan ships were sighted in Trinidadian waters just off the mainland. Prime Minister Williams had reportedly requested the arms which the ships delivered to the government. Meanwhile, the country was experiencing a number of strikes in different industries, even though they had been outlawed in 1965 by the Industrial Stabilization Act. There were calls for "Power to the People" as well as demands to the government to end unemployment and to effectively cut off foreign domination of the economy.

One of the most active Black Power organizations in the Caribbean was the Guyana-based African Society for Cultural Relations with Independent Africa (ASCRIA) under the leadership of Eusi Kwayana. While ASCRIA supported Burnham's nationalization of Demba, it believed that "nationalization without workers' control and workers' self-management is a fraud."[45] In 1970, in opposition to the highly bureaucratized leadership of the Guyana Mine Workers Union (BMWU), ASCRIA spearheaded a strike by bauxite mine workers that began as a protest calling for protection of the black nurses at a mining location. The workers demanded protection for black women against white men, but this escalated to include demands for a pay hike which the workers had been promised the previous summer. The strike occurred in the midst of negotiations between the government and the Demerara Bauxite Company to settle issues related to the nationalization of the company.

Whatever the inadequacies and limitations of Black Power and other movements which appeared on the scene in the late 1960s and early 1970s, it marked a repudiation of the existing development model and a major challenge to the prevailing political economy.

Government Responses and the
Evolving International Political Economy

The most immediate and pervasive response of area governments to Black Power uprisings was to stop the demonstrations and repress activity which posed a threat to the maintenance of national order or to the operation of foreign institutions which might be targets of attack. In Jamaica and Trinidad, the police attacked the marchers first, usually before property damage had taken place. Some demonstrators were killed. In Trinidad and Tobago the government detained a number of people suspected to be Black Power

62

leaders. The government found it necessary to request from the United States the delivery of arms and the presence of the U.S. Navy.

Prime Minister Williams' government did, however, take steps to appease the Black Power Movement. During the uprisings he announced a 5% special tax levy on companies to be used to combat unemployment and warned businesses against racial discrimination in hiring.[46] During the 1971 national elections, issues were forced into categories which indicated either a commitment to the "new politics" or to the Westminster model. The PNM (People's National Movement—Williams' party) in its election manifesto presented proposals for changing the electoral law and administration. They proposed reduction of the voting age to eighteen, changing the governmental system from a monarchy to a republic, introducing a cooperative sector to reduce the dependence on foreign capital and ownership and increasing participation of nationals in the ownership and control of industrial enterprises.[47] Moreover, in response to accusations against Canadian and U.S. banks of discrimination in hiring and loan policy, the Trinidadian government established the National Commercial Bank in 1971 and ordered all state agencies to bank with it. The government also assisted in the formation of manufacturing and commercial cooperatives.[48] As a first step toward full ownership, it took over forty-nine percent interest in the Tate & Lyle sugar company in Trinidad. Later, it raised taxes on the profits of the oil companies operating in the country.

A general response of local Caribbean governments has been to incorporate Black Power rhetoric into government propaganda. There are references to "Power to the People" in publications concerning foreign economic control and dependence on foreign capital. Some efforts have been made to institute policies requiring joint ventures for new and old corporate operations. In fact, the Trinagoan government announced in 1972 that in certain key sectors, no new 100% foreign-owned ventures would be permitted. The question is, however, have substantive efforts been made to restructure the political economy of these countries.

Specific governmental actions aimed at the political economy occurred at various levels. One approach was to raise the revenue-extracting potential *vis-à-vis* the firms by increasing taxation. It has also been used by Guyana in the Booker sugar holdings, but the approach was used most aggressively by Jamaica with respect to the bauxite and alumina companies. Jamaica established a production levy that multiplied several-fold its revenue from bauxite. This method has been most common in the natural resources sector.

A more widely used approach is localization or participation: reducing the number of expatriates in the multinationals and other foreign firms and opening up positions for local people, a method used in all sectors. The principal meaning of localization, however, is the acquisition of equity in the firms by local individuals, associations, unions, or government. This has been used mostly in Jamaica and Trinidad, especially in the banking and manufacturing sectors. Of course, it is often a complete sham, especially in banking; banks can double the price of shares before selling, thereby lose nothing, and therefore retain control. One variant of participation is government partnership in joint ventures, such as Jamaica with Alcoa, and Trinidad and Tobago with Texaco.

A more drastic approach is nationalization. Partial nationalization with compensation was at first used by Trinidad with the sugar multinational Tate & Lyle, which became Acroni Ltd. Selective full nationalization can also be used, such as when a subsidiary is fully bought up while the rest of that particular sector is left untouched. Guyana nationalized Demba in 1971 with full compensation to be paid from revenues over a period of years with interest after an initial down payment. It was not until 1975 that the other bauxite company, Reynolds, was acquired.

Another form of selective nationalization could be called staggered nationalization, such as when Jamaica acquires multinational-owned sugar land for cane growing (the least profitable aspect of the business) without touching the other aspects. This is a good way for the multinational to rid itself of the least productive and most uncertain part of the operation, unloading thousands of workers and a whole set of industrial relations problems in the process. The acquisition of the surface right to the land held by the bauxite multinationals in the second stage of its plan to take over the industry is another form of staggered nationalization on the part of the Jamaican government. The next step is purported to be acquisition of subsoil rights, to be followed by partial equity acquisition in the operation, crowned by full equity acquisition over time.

Only Guyana has achieved the full nationalization of its natural resources sector, with the acquisition of the Jessel sugar holding in 1975 and of the Booker McConnell holdings, after 160 years, on April 26, 1976—the 10th anniversary of independence—for G$102.5 million. For British Guyana, once called Booker's Guiana, that is indeed the end of an era.

Trinidad has acquired Shell with its 100,000 barrel-a-day refinery, but not Texaco, with its 300,000 bpd-capacity refinery. Texaco and the Trinidadian government have projected various joint ventures in the petrochemical field. Trinidad also acquired the marketing outlets of British Petroleum (BP) on its territory.

In the tourist industry, Caribbean governments, even in such overly tourist-dependent countries as the Bahamas, have been quietly buying international hotels. The process is most advanced in Jamaica. In June 1976 the government arranged to purchase the Holiday Inn at Montego Bay for $J11.8 million; it has also decided to buy a major share in the Pegasus Hotel in New Kingston.[49]

Another level of action is that of regional cooperation beyond the regular activities of the Caribbean Common Market (CARICOM) and Caribbean Economic Community. Some of the activities involve West Indian governments alone. One category concerns projects of joint ventures, such as the aluminum smelter project between Jamaica, Guyana, and Trinidad, where the latter would provide the substantial energy needed through its considerable reserves of natural gas, while the other two would provide the bauxite and alumina. One category recently added to the new intra-Carribean political economy is financial assistance. Jamaica, which in spite of its 1974 windfall from increased revenues from bauxite and sugar, faced in 1976 a dangerous balance of payment situation, a declining rate of production, and a high rate of inflation. In the course of an emergency "Big Four" summit meeting that year with Trinidad, Guyana, and Barbados, a complex loan of $J80 million (Trinidad and Tobago contributed $J70 million, Barbados $J7 million, and Guyana $J3 million) was granted to remedy the situation.[50]

In the larger Caribbean area, there are various joint projects such as Jamaican-Mexican and Jamaican-Venezuelan alumina and aluminum smelters. In both cases, Jamaica will supply the bauxite and the other partner the energy through petroleum. The overall purpose is to establish an integrated regional bauxite complex that includes Surinam.

On an extra-regional level, the most directly relevant action has been the creation of the International Bauxite Association (IBA) in which Jamaica has played the leadership role. The headquarters are in Kingston and the chief executive officer is a Guyanese. It is not another OPEC, because it faces a less oligopolistic market and the producers are less politically homogeneous, but it has potential. Also of relevance is the active role of the Caribbean governments in ACP (African, Caribbean, and Pacific Group), whose current President of the Council of Ministers is Guyana's Minister of Trade, George King.

Conclusion

All these measures have been taken in a political framework which, especially for Jamaica and Guyana, is self-consciously radical at the international level. All three countries were among the first to reestablish relations with Cuba. Since then, there have been increasing exchanges between Jamaica and Guyana on the one hand, and Cuba on the other.

Internally both governments have proclaimed themselves to be socialist: democratic socialism in Jamaica and cooperative socialism in Guyana. However, there are varying concepts of socialism. Burnham in Guyana declared himself for Marxism-Leninism, and Manley of Jamaica has been quoted several times as having said in January 1976, "I could never be a Communist. I am a profoundly democratic person."[51] As a result of international pressures, both countries have complained of efforts to destabilize their economies, an oft-repeated cry in which Barbados has also joined. This prompted the United States government to make the statement that it "has complete respect for the sovereignty of other nations and for the right of other peoples to freely select their own political and economic systems."[52]

A healthy dose of paranoia is not the only thing that these governments have acquired from their attempts at system change. They have enlarged and diversified international contacts and involvement thereby affecting their foreign policy options. New experiences in economic diplomacy have been acquired through negotiations with multinationals. New skills and new bureaucratic tools and agencies, such as Jamaica's National Bauxite Commission, have been developed.[53] While doing this, the governments keep their eyes on the Left. In Guyana, the established Left was forced to join in, temporarily frustrating hopes of the nonestablished Left for a racist-free grand Leftist coalition for revolutionary change.

Has there, then, been marked system change? There have been modifications. There is greater national ownership of natural resources, especially in Guyana, though in return for compensations, marketing, and other agreements favorable to the corporations. A higher rate of revenue is flowing from foreign investment. The manufacturing sector, however, has not been touched seriously; the model of industrialization by invitation prevails, although there are now locally controlled banking facilities capable of servicing the local corporate class.

The relations of power have been modified, but not drastically, facilitated largely by the international climate. The activities of OPEC and its members, for example, were important: the announcement of renegotiation of bauxite contracts by Jamaica in November 1973 came in the same month that OPEC announced its price increase and its potential for nearly tripling Jamaica's oil expenditures from 1973 to 1974. Some of the Caribbean measures, however, such as the nationalization of Demba and the partial nationalization of Tate

& Lyle, antedated the activist stage of OPEC. But other Caribbean countries—Haiti, the Dominican Republic, and Surinam, all bauxite exporters—were exposed to the same international events, and none of them has gone beyond benefiting from higher taxation in following Jamaica's lead. Clearly, internal socio-political dynamics are crucial.

In Guyana, the relentless and long-standing pressures of the old Left, combined with Black Power and the new Left, pushed Burnham continuously and effectively to the Left. In Jamaica, the disturbances of the turn of the decade coincided with the coming to power of Michael Manley, a master of the new politics, riding on a wave of high expectations, following a decade of stagnation with the JLP. In Trinidad, the autocratic Dr. Williams and his PNM were temporarily jolted out of their own stagnation in 1970, but the so-called 1970 Revolution was no revolution at all, and while Williams has been engaging in system manipulation too, the ineffectualness of the Left, together with the considerable revenues from oil, have allowed him to avoid moving as far as Manley and Burnham. It may be, though, that with the rise of the United Labor Front as the major opposition party in Parliament, the rules of the game will change.

FOOTNOTES

1. Eric Williams, *Capitalism and Slavery,* New York: Capricorn Books, 1966.

2. Pan American Union, *Plantation Systems of the New World,* Washington, D.C.: P.A.U., 1959; George L. Beckford, *Persistent Poverty: Underdevelopment in Plantation Economies of the Third World,* New York: Oxford University Press, 1972; and Lloyd Best, "Outlines of a Model of Pure Plantation Economy," *Social and Economic Studies* Vol. 17, No. 3, September 1968.

3. George L. Beckford, *op. cit.,* Chaps. 4 and 5.

4. Peter Phillips, "Jamaican Foreign Relations and National Capitalism— Some Research Notes and Perspectives," Annual Meeting of the African Heritage Studies Association, Atlanta, Georgia, April 22-25, 1976.

5. Louis Lindsay, *The Myth of Independence: Middle Class Politics and Non-Mobilization in Jamaica,* Working Paper, No. 6, Institute of Social and Economic Research, University of the West Indies, Mona, Jamaica, 1975: 49. See also Trevor Munroe, *The Politics of Constitutional Decolonization: Jamaica, 1944-62,* Mona: Institute of Social and Economic Research, University of the West Indies, 1972.

6. Hilbourne A. Watson, "Nationalism and Socialism in the Commonwealth Caribbean: Aspects of Contemporary Politics and Political Economy," Annual Meeting of the National Conference of Black Political Scientists, Chicago, Illinois, April 29-May 1, 1976, especially pp. 5-8.

7. Fernando Henrique Cardoso, "The Consumption of Dependency Theory in the U.S.," Annual Meeting of the Latin American Studies Association, Atlanta, Georgia, March 25-28, 1976: 24.

8. Wendell Bell and Ivar Oxaal, *Decisions of Nationhood: Political and Social Development in the British Caribbean,* The Social Science Foundation and Department of International Relations, Monograph Series in World Affairs, Nos. 3 and 4, University of Denver, Denver, Colorado, 1963-64: 40.

9. *Ibid.,* 38.

10. G. Beckford, *op. cit.*

11. Ann Spackman, "The Role of Private Companies in the Politics of Empire: A Case Study of Bauxite and Diamond Companies in Guyana in the Early 1920's," *Social and Economic Studies,* Vol. 24, No. 3, September 1975: 341-378.

12. *Ibid.*

13. G.E. Cumper, "Dependence, Development and the Sociology of Economic Thought," *Social and Economic Studies,* Vol. 23, No. 3, September 1974: 466.

14. The size variable plays an important role in Caribbean economic literature. See, for instance, William G. Demas, *The Economics of Development in Small*

Countries with Special Reference to the Caribbean, Montreal: McGill University Press, 1965; Lloyd Best, "Size and Survival," *New World, Guyana Independence Issue,* 1966: 58; and Steve De Castro, "The Effects of Modern Technology on Small Developing Countries with Surplus Labour," *Caribbean Quarterly,* Vol. 12, No. 3, 1966. For a different perspective see Clive Y. Thomas, *Dependence and Transformation: The Economics of the Transition to Socialism,* New York: Monthly Review Press, 1974, esp. Chap. 2.

15. See W. Arthur Lewis, "The Industrialization of Puerto Rico," *Caribbean Economic Review,* Vol. 1, Nos. 1 and 2, 1949; "The Industrialization of the British West Indies," *Caribbean Economic Review,* Vol. 2, 1950; *Jamaica's Economic Problems,* Kingston, Jamaica: Gleaner Company Pamphlet, 1964.

16. G.E. Cumper, *op. cit.,* 465-466. This is a critique of Norman Girvan, "The Development of Dependency Economics in the Caribbean and Latin America: Review and Comparison," *Social and Economic Studies,* Vol. 22, No. 1, March 1973: 1-33.

17. Steve De Castro, *Tax Holidays for Industry: Why We Have to Abolish Them and How to Do It,* Pamphlet No. 8, New World Group, Mona, Kingston, Jamaica, March 1973.

18. Norman Girvan, "Making the Rules of the Game: Company-Country Agreements in the Bauxite Industry," *Social and Economic Studies,* XX, No. 4, December 1971: 386-390.

19. *Ibid.,* 386, 398-406.

20. *Ibid.,* 386, 407-411.

21. *Ibid.,* 386.

22. Dale L. Johnson, "Dependence and the International System" in J.D. Cockcroft, A.G. Frank and D.L. Johnson, *Dependence and Underdevelopment: Latin America's Political Economy,* Garden City, New York: Doubleday, 1972: 85.

23. Girvan, *op. cit.,* 405.

24. *Ibid.,* 406.

25. Selwyn Ryan, "Restructuring the Trinidad Economy" in Norman Girvan and Owen Jefferson, eds., *Readings in the Political Economy of the Caribbean,* 1st ed., Mona: New World, 1971: 188.

26. *Ibid.,* 189.

27. Owen Jefferson, "Some Aspects of the Post-War Economic Development of Jamaica," in Girvan and Jefferson, *op. cit.,* 112.

28. Norman Girvan, "Why We Need to Nationalize Bauxite and How," *ibid.,* 220.

29. Havelock Brewster, "The Social Economy of Sugar," *ibid.,* 53.

30. Norman Girvan, *Aspects of the Political Economy of Race in the Caribbean and in the Americas,* Working Paper, No. 7, Institute of Social and Economic Research, University of the West Indies, Mona, Jamaica, 1975, especially pp. 24-31.

31. Maurice St. Pierre, ''Race, the Political Factor and the Nationalization of the Demerara Bauxite Company, Guyana,'' *Social and Economic Studies,* Vol. 24, No. 4, December 1975: 481-502.

32. For a recent and informative study of the Rastas, see Avarita L. Hanson, *The Rastafarians of Kingston, Jamaica: A Movement in Search of a New Social Order,* honors thesis, Harvard University, Cambridge, Massachusetts, 1975.

33. *Sunday Express* (Trinidad), May 23, 1976: 1; *Sunday Guardian,* May 23, 1976: 1.

For a sympathetic portrait of Lloyd Best's political activism, see Ivar Oxaal, ''The Dependency Economist as Grassroot Politician,'' in Ivar Oxaal, Tony Barnett and David Booth, eds., *Beyond the Sociology of Development,* Boston: Routledge and Kegan Paul, 1965: 28-49.

34. ''A Working Class Party in Trinago,'' *Race Today,* Vol. 8, No. 2, February 1976: 33. See also ''ULF Forms Working Class Party,'' *Caribbean Dialogue,* Vol. 2, No. 1, January 1976: 2-3.

35. Lloyd Best, *Black Power and National Reconstruction: Proposals Following the February Revolution,* March 19, 1970, pamphlet, Tapia House, Tunapuna, May 3, 1974: 12.

36. Interview with James Millette, Mona, Jamaica, July 10, 1974.

37. See, for instance, Bukka Rennie, *History of the Working-Class in the 20th Century–Trinidad and Tobago,* Toronto: New Beginning Movement, 1974.

38. A protest demonstration against the Canadian trial of West Indian students charged with participating in the burning down of the Computer Center at Sir George Williams University in Montreal started the Trinidad Black Power revolt of 1970.

39. *Manifesto of the URO: Socialism and Liberation,* Port of Spain, December 31, 1972: 33-40.

40. Cheddi Jagan, ''Critical Support,'' *Caribbean Dialogue,* Vol. 1, No. 3, November/December 1975: 17.

41. Interview, Mona, Jamaica, July 5, 1974.

42. This was repeatedly stated by respondents in Mona, Jamaica in July 1974.

43. Walter Rodney, *The Groundings With My Brothers,* London: Boyle L'Ouverture Publications, 1969: 16, 18.

44. Student-Staff Action Committee, ''Diary of Events for October 16, 1968: Protest in Kingston Over the Banning of Dr. Walter Rodney,'' in Trevor Munroe and

Rupert Lewis, eds., *Readings in the Government and Politics of the West Indies,* Mona, Dept. of Government, University of the West Indies, 1971: 209.

45. Eusi Kwayana, *The Bauxite Strike and the Old Politics,* Georgetown, Guyana, 1972: 13.

46. Ivar Oxaal, *Race and Revolutionary Consciousness: An Existential Report on the 1970 Black Power Revolt in Trinidad,* Cambridge, Mass.: Schenkman, 1971: 23.

47. Edward Greene, ''An Analysis of the General Elections in Trinidad and Tobago 1971,'' in Munroe and Lewis, *op. cit.,* 140.

48. *New York Times,* February 28, 1972.

49. *The Jamaica Weekly Gleaner,* June 22, 1976: 27.

50. *Ibid.,* 1, 4, 6.

51. *Ibid.,* 6.

52. *Ibid.,* 1.

53. See a perceptive analysis in Locksley G. E. Edmonson, ''Bauxite Diplomacy in the Caribbean and in International Relations: A Preliminary Exploration,'' Paper read at the Annual Meeting of the International Studies Association, Toronto, Canada, February 24-28, 1976.

THE GLOBAL CORPORATION, ETHNO-NATIONALISM AND THE CHANGING FACE OF THE WESTERN EUROPEAN STATE

Phillip M. Rawkins

Introduction

In contemporary Western Europe two apparently contradictory forces of great historical moment are at work: a trend towards transnational cooperation in political and economic matters, and a re-emergence of territorial sectionalism and nationalism in geographically and culturally peripheral regions of states previously thought to be successfully integrated. It is generally recognized that the two developments are related, but there is disagreement as to the character of the relationship.

Some dismiss the resurgence of nationalism among Basques, Bretons, Welsh, Scots, and Walloons as an unfortunate anachronism, irrelevant and damaging to the march towards European unification. In terms of this perspective, the nation-state has had its day: for long-submerged national minorities to claim the right of self-determination is absurd. More sympathetic observers, however, have perceived in such movements an assertion of human values, values thought to be threatened by the growing power of centralized political bureaucracies and global business corporations.

Unfortunately, neither interpretation provides much insight into the complexity of the processes of social and economic change which have produced the new wave of nationalist feeling. This paper offers an explanation of the phenomenon in terms of the changing character of the relationship between international economic institutions, the nation-state, and the populations currently undergoing mobilization on what Walker Connor has termed an "ethno-nationalist" basis.[1]

Nationalism and Uneven Development

To accept the argument that nationalism is best understood as a natural phenomenon, or an historical coming of age meeting a universally-felt need, is to fall prey to a romantic interpretation of history. As Elie Kedourie has pointed out, "nationalism is a doctrine invented in Europe at the beginning of the 19th century."[2] However, there may well be powerful factors— economic, social and political—which make the nationalist idea appear a natural and irresistable response to historical developments.[3]

Nineteenth century European nationalism is best viewed as a response to the development and diffusion of the modern, capitalist, industrial economy.

Despite the assumptions of the linear conception of progress, in nineteenth century Europe—as in colonial Asia and Africa a century later—the impact of modernization has been highly uneven in terms of its geographical effect. As a result, nationalist history has been characterized by an erratic procession of local nationalisms, as the institutions and agencies of the modern economy touched particular regions at particular times in particular ways.

Nationalism has always and everywhere had an ambivalent character: part carrier of modernity, and part symbol of reaction against economic modernization and the concept of progress. Overwhelmed by the force of capitalist expansion, the elites of peripheral regions have sought to resist such expansion, while simultaneously harnessing its forces for their own advantage.[4]

Hence, nationalism is both unifying and divisive. In its nonimperialist variant, nationalism may be understood as the compensatory ideology of peoples relatively distant, culturally and geographically, from the centres of capital concentration. Such peoples experience the disorder brought about by economic change, but find themselves unable to enjoy its promised benefits to the full.

The emergence of regional discontent and ethno-nationalist opposition to the maintenance of the structure of modern nation-states may be similarly related to the processes of uneven development. However, in the context of advanced industrial-technological society, the relationship is one of considerable intricacy, requiring specification of intervening variables.

Technological advance in transportation, in communications, and in the production process has facilitated enormous developments in what Max Weber termed the "rationalization" of economic life.[5] Increasingly, technology is integrated with the forces of production in the global corporation, diversifying investment in many industries in many countries. Through technological change, capital investment is increasingly concentrated in metropolitan regions, and in the hands of an ever-decreasing number of vertically—and horizontally—integrated companies.[6] A multi-national system of trade and payments is emerging; an expanding volume of trade is conducted between the same firms in different countries.

Despite the growing uniformity of social and cultural patterns throughout the territory of the nation-state, recent decades have not seen the achievement of economic integration as measured by the development of a balanced, geographically-diversified economic system. In an earlier phase of industrial growth, the peripheral regions of Western Europe were characterized by an unbalanced, nondiversified industrial profile and by considerable division between their rural and urban sectors. Recent trends have brought a renewed drain of capital from the hinterland towards the metropolis, putting additional strains in the social fabric of the periphery.

The expansion of heavy industry in the late nineteenth century resulted in a massive increase in demand for labour. By contrast, corporate growth results in an increasing rate of capital investment per worker. Associated with this trend is the growing significance of technological innovation—as compared with the surplus value of labour productivity over labour cost—as a basis for profitability. A sharp division of labour has been created between a concentrated, high-wage, technologically advanced, highly productive industrial core in Western Europe, North American, and Japan—and a more extensive, low wage, low technology and low productivity sector in the less developed countries.[7]

In such circumstances, the economic advantages have disappeared in West European regions whose economies were dependent upon a small range of extractive and heavy manufacturing industries—hence the economic difficulties of the Walloon south of Belgium, South Wales, the Scottish Clydeside, and the Belfast area of Northern Ireland. Despite substantial financial inducements offered by national governments, major national and international corporations are reluctant to invest in peripheral areas.[8] The result is high unemployment, emigration of the young, and breakdown of communities and established social structures.

Similarly, the relative poverty of rural areas of the periphery—such as the interior and west coast of Brittany, the French Basque Country, Galicia, Corsica, Southern Italy, the Scottish Highland interior, and central Wales— has been exacerbated. Such areas have little prospect of a viable economic future. The chief function of their populations is to act as a territorial reserve labour pool, or as service employees maintaining a summer playground for the wealthy.[9] Though the agencies of the welfare state may assist these casualties of economic progress by attempting to equalize incomes on a geographical basis, such efforts are limited: the efforts merely compensate for an imbalance, the source of which is built into the system, and whose impact will continue to be felt. Young people, for example, are obliged to leave in search of work. Those fortunate enough to find employment locally are priced out of the housing market by city-based purchasers of second homes.

The extraordinary growth of the communications network in Western Europe since 1945 brought awareness of a wider world to the peoples of the periphery and exposed them to culturally homogenizing values. Inclusion in the educational and communications systems of the nation-state led to intensified pressures towards assimilation of culturally distinctive populations. But, when combined with the failure of the state to combat uneven development, these changes may produce a heightened social awareness of real or idealized cultural distinctiveness and a broad sense of relative deprivation.

In such circumstances there may emerge a reevaluation of personal identity and political loyalty.[10] Caught between two worlds, the educated young may come to appreciate the values of their own cultural milieu precisely when offered the opportunity to leave it. They may also conclude that the survival of the indigenous culture and society is threatened by the social forces of the metropolitan world, and may seek to define their own identity in a struggle against the intruder. For others the situation may be less dramatic. But to the citizens of the periphery—rural and urban—national governments appear ineffective in their ability to meet popular expectations, and to form policies in accord with local needs and sensitivities. The repercussions of uneven economic development bring together those whose initial concerns are primarily cultural, and those whose demands are basically economic. As capital becomes increasingly international in nature, government ability to control the course of events, and to meet the special needs of its peripheral regions and cultural minorities, declines.[11]

The Global Corporation and the Advanced Industrial State

To understand the state's failure to combat the impact of uneven development, it is necessary to consider those factors which have led to a transformation of the state's role in the world economic system. The internationalization of capital concentration and economic enterprise has brought about more than a structural transformation of the nation-state to influence events. As Barnet and Müller have commented:

> Loss of control over money, increasing concentration of income and wealth, failure to maintain employment, and mounting debts are symptoms of the permanent managerial crisis that now afflicts advanced industrial societies as well as poor countries. . . . Territorially-based government lacks the imagination and the power to develop a political response to the dynamic global economic forces which, more and more, are shaping our lives.[12]

Paradoxically, the power of the state *vis-à-vis* the citizen and the encroachment of the state bureaucracies on day-to-day life has grown considerably in recent decades. The internationalization of capital has not suppressed the state. It has, rather, increased its difficulties in performing its role as manager and guarantor of full employment, social peace, and political consensus. The power of international capital can provide incentive and help the state achieve its general goals. Though conflicts of interest have emerged between nation-states and global corporations, the general trend has been towards cooperation.[13] The result has been a decline in the state's ability to plan and pursue its own destiny.

As Stephen Hymer has pointed out, the array of governmental policy instruments (monetary, fiscal, and wage) becomes progressively less effective the more open the economy and the greater the proportion of foreign investment.[14] The concentration of capital, technology, and scientific expertise in the hands of global corporations makes it essential for governments to meet the terms presented by international capital as a means of promoting economic growth and maintaining relatively high levels of employment.[15] The Chrysler Corporation extracted a massive subsidy from the British Government in 1976 in exchange for continuing production at its Scottish plant. For the government to have refused to meet such humiliating conditions would have resulted in substantial unemployment and yet another electoral issue for the Scottish National Party.

The European Economic Community has been viewed by many as a means to improve the competitive power of European corporations *vis-à-vis* their international rivals. Ironically, the international corporations have gained most from the creation of the tariff-free market. They have been able to apply the benefits of scale already enjoyed in domestic and world markets to a new arena of production and marketing. Hence they enjoy substantial advantages over the majority of European corporations, further increasing their global dominance and their ability to play off one nation-state against another.[16] It is the adaptation of the state to the international corporate system, and an acceptance of the system's values—not a literal transfer of powers to transnational economic and political institutions—which has reduced the state's ability to cope with ruptures in national unity.[17]

The West European state has become dependent for its prosperity on the maintenance of the international system, and hence on centralization of capital, technology, and affluence. The peripheral regions cannot expect relief within the existing political framework. Hence, solutions to their problems presuppose a rejection of prevailing political structures and values. The question of values is particularly significant, as is emphasized by Kari Levitt in her essay on Canada, Quebec, and the multi-national corporation:

> Underdevelopment, be it of Canada or Quebec, is perpetuated above all by our collective mentality of dependence and impotence with respect to the supposed superiority of the economic, political and even the cultural institutions of the dominant metropolis. It follows that the first step towards and escape from underdevelopment and hinterland status is the self-definition and self-assertion of a society in its own terms.[18]

77

The Significance of Culture and the Challenge of Minority Nationalism

Nationalism is not simply a romantic variant of regionalism. It would be erroneous to comprehend the emergence of minority nationalist movements on the European periphery in terms of a demand for regional planning and a demand for redistribution of the benefits of growth. The dimension of values, of culture and thus of ethnic identity is all-important. To understand this, the nature of the broader impact of the international corporate order must be clarified.

As has been argued above, the impact of economic change and hence of social disruption has been particularly marked on the periphery. One consequence has been a modification in the role of culture, defined by Ernest Gellner as "the manner in which one communicates in the broadest sense."[19] Generally, culture reinforces social structure, and its forms symbolize and emphasize the character of the substance of existing structures.

As established social structures undergo disruption and transformation, the link between structure and cultures is broken. Normally, an individual finds identity through a place in the social structure; the identity, in turn, is symbolized and reinforced in culture. In transitional society, Gellner argues, culture replaces social structure as the realm for definition of identities. Individual roles fail to accord with individual self-perceptions. Hence a person's culture—style of conduct and expression—becomes the identity, and there exist the circumstances under which individuals may come to classify themselves self-consciously according to nationality.[20] Such considerations arise from the ill-effects brought about by capital and technology concentration and resulting uneven development in the European periphery. The effects of social disruption, then, become concentrated on the historical and cultural faultlines of what have always been multi-ethnic societies.[21] As social structures and institutions are undermined by the impact of external forces, so have cultural and historical symbols emphasizing ethnic distinctiveness become increasingly significant as a focus for personal identity.

Uneven development tends to stimulate ethnic awareness while undermining social indicators of ethnic diversity—hence the common phenomenon of renewed interest in indigenous cultural forms, languages, national history, and rural traditions among the educated, urbanized young of Western European national minorities.[22] As Ernest Gellner has put it, "the self-image of nationalism involves the stress of folk, folk-lore, popular culture, etc.—in fact, nationalism becomes important precisely when these things become artificial."[23]

In seeking to carry out political mobilization on the basis of culture and ethnic identity, the nationalist movements, according to Weber, are standing

78

against the "rationalization" of the modern world. Through this concept Weber was attempting to express and explain the effects of scientific-technical progress on the institutional arrangements of societies undergoing "modernization." Essentially, he perceived an everexpanding application of analytically based scientific-technical rules to production and bureaucratic administration.[24]

In the current period, the progress of rationalization is associated with the dominance of the global corporation, and the application of scientific and technical knowledge to all forms of social and economic activity by business and state bureaucracies. As the chief carrier of rationalization, the multi-national corporation's goal is to create a world in which economic activity can be carried on with maximum efficiency. The achievement of social peace, cultural uniformity, and political order would facilitate the establishment of a "global shopping center" in which differences in taste and consumption patterns would be based solely on different levels of purchasing power, and which would result in the emergence of the "world customer."[25]

From this perspective, nationalism, national frontiers, and ethnic consciousness can be perceived only as irrational elements to be dispelled by the forces of reason. According to Jacques Maisonrouge of IBM, the global corporation is a vehicle of enlightenment which "has introduced rationality into international and human relations" and has reduced "the emotional and haphazard elements of life."[26] Clearly, there is little possibility of peaceful coexistence between ethno-nationalism and the global corporation. However, as has been argued above, the major West European states have accommodated themselves to the new international order, and domestic politics have been transformed accordingly. While established national frontiers and cultural patterns necessitate extensive market research and product development analysis, they can hardly be said to form a serious barrier to the dominance of the international corporate system.

Of crucial significance in the trend towards homogenization of culture is control of communications networks by the global corporations and their accomplices, the state bureaucracies. In seeking to oppose the dissemination of international mass culture, ethno-nationalists must attack the control of media input and distribution. Broadcasting, education, and language rights are areas of bitterly divisive political conflict in Brittany, Wales, Quebec, and the French and Spanish Basque country. A degree of local control of media input in Wales, in Scotland, and to a much greater extent in Quebec has undoubtedly had a substantial effect on ethnic awareness in recent years.

Rationalization in the sphere of government and politics is associated with the power of technical control in administration and with an application of scientific-technical expertise to the policy-making process. In these terms, politics becomes an arena of practical or technical problems, and political choices are seen to revolve around criteria of efficiency rather than of morality. With the dominance of the technocratic ethos, traditional ideologies and the political alternatives they offer become outmoded; political action is guided by technical rules rather than by societal norms.[27] The overall trend is towards depoliticization: an increasing proportion of the subject matter of politics is deemed appropriate for expert deliberation rather than public debate, and thus is concerned with decisions over means rather than ends.

Ethno-nationalism may be seen as opposition to a trend where politics becomes just one aspect of a general process of socialization into passive adaptation to the growing power of technical control.[28] It stands against a form of politics in which there is a reluctance to acknowledge difference of interest, to perceive the relevance of alternative value perspectives, or to allow the adequate expression of dissent with political choices.[29] The popular appeal of the politics of ethnic identity underscores the failure of the political system to fulfill spiritual and/or moral needs. It may also be seen as a rejection of the preoccupation in state decision-making with a technocratic rationality which obscures both the conflict of economic interests and the salience of a broad range of human needs to the achievement of societal well-being.

Conclusion

Max Weber's attitude to rationalization was ambivalent.[30] He saw it associated with the development of modern rational capitalism, the most advanced economic system yet developed by man, and he saw the potential for the confinement of man's individual creativity and autonomy within the "iron cage" of bureaucracy in the rationalization of social activity which had facilitated the emergence of modern capitalism in the first place.[31]

Weber's nightmare of the iron cage represents a situation in which the means of societal action become ends, and in which technocratic consciousness becomes an overarching ideology. In such circumstances, distinct interests do not disappear; rather, they become masked, and the society becomes subject to manipulation by those controlling economic life. The global corporation is perhaps a potential realization of Weber's fears, combining technical advance and an expansion of society's productive powers with a broad threat to human liberty and to the scope of expression of collective and individual creativity.

In order to combat bureaucratization of everyday life, an offsetting form of rationalization should occur in the sphere of social interaction and culture.

Jurgen Habermas sees this development in the removal of restrictions on communication, allowing open public discussion on principles of societal action and norms to govern human conduct.[32] This brings us back to Gellner's point concerning the enhanced salience of culture in circumstances of transition. Gellner argues that culture becomes the only medium for establishing individual and collective identity; Habermas argues that the opening-up of the process of communication is the only means towards the achievement of an endogenous *social rationalization* and and which is hence a means towards human liberation. Culture and communications, then, form the context in which reassertion of the political dimension and reorientation of individual identity must occur. Together, the two processes fulfill the moral and spiritual needs—of belonging and self-actualization, in Maslow's terms—necessarily neglected in a system dominated by the technocratic ethos.[33]

The phenomenon of ethno-nationalism represents an important form of positive opposition to the growing power of a morally uninformed technical control. Despite occasional propagandistic excesses of language, incidences of emotive chauvinism, and the obvious existence of substantial differences in the ideologies of the various movements, the logic of ethno-nationalism places it firmly in opposition to the global corporation. The focus on culture and ethnic identity represents a demand for a society in which human purpose might be democratically defined and the actions of economic and political institutions made amenable to political control. In such a society there would exist a coincidence of political and cultural identity, symbolizing a relationship of balance as between the two modes of rationalization.[34]

Ethno-nationalism is more than electoral politics, even though leaders of successful West European Nationalist parties are not immune to the influence of economic rationalization and the technocratic ethos. The ethno-nationalist movements are vastly broader in scope than the political parties which attempt to harness their strength. In both Scotland and Quebec, though nationalist politicians may seek to appease and reassure international capital, the broader social movements push, via demands for local control of cultural institutions and communications, in the direction of an opening rather than a closure of political debate.

FOOTNOTES

1. Walker Connor, "Nation-Building or Nation-Destroying?" *World Politics,* Vol. 24, 3, April, 1972: 319-355; also Connor, "The Politics of Ethnonationalism," *Journal of International Affairs,* Vol. 27, 1, 1973: 1-21.

2. Elie Kedourie, *Nationalism,* London: Hutchinson, 1960: 9.

3. Ernest Gellner, *Thought and Change,* London: Weidenfeld and Nicholson, 1964: 150-1.

4. See Tom Nairn, "The Modern Janus," *New Left Review,* 94, November-December, 1975: 12; more generally, see Anthony D. Smith, *Theories of Nationalism,* London: Duckworth, 1971.

5. See Hans Gerth and C. Wright Mills, eds., *From Max Weber: Essays in Sociology,* London: Routledge, 1948: 51-55, 196-244.

6. For a detailed examination of these developments, see Nicos Poulantzas, "Internationalization of Capitalist Relations and the Nation-State," *Economy and Society,* Vol. 3, 2, May 1974: 145-179; Ernest Mandel, *Europe versus America: Contradictions of Imperialism,* London: new Left Books, 1970, and Mandel, *Capitalism and Regional Disparities,* Toronto: New Hogtown Press, 1973; Kari Levitt, *Silent Surrender: The Multinational Corporation in Canada,* Toronto: Macmillan, 1970; Stephen Hymer, "The Multinational Corporation and the Law of Uneven Development," in J.N. Bhagwati, ed., *Economics and World Order from the 1970's to the 1990's,* New York: Macmillan, 1972: 113-140.

7. See Hymer, op. cit., 119-120; also Stuart Holland, *The Socialist Challenge,* London: Quartet Books, 1975: 109-110.

8. For an examination of the factors responsible for the failure of regional policy in Western Europe, and a consideration of some British case-studies, see Holland, *op. cit.,* 75-110; more generally, see Poulantzas, *op. cit.,* 177-179, and Mandel "Regional Disparities," *op. cit.,* section 3.

9. For documentation of these trends, see, for example: Ian Carter, "The Highlands of Scotland as an Underdeveloped Region," paper read at *British Sociological Association,* Annual conference, 1972; Patricia Elton Mayo, *The Roots of Identity,* London: Allen Lane, the Penguin Press, 1974; "Strangers at the Feast: A Survey of the Development Regions of the EEC," *Economist,* January 25, 1975, supplement; Bart Milner, "The French Far West," *New Society,* October 25, 1973: 197-8; three in-depth articles in *Le Monde,* English section on Corsica, September 6 and 27, 1975, June 6, 1976; P.M. Rawkins, *Minority Nationalism and the Advanced Industrial State: A Case-study of Contemporary Wales,* unpublished Ph.D. Dissertation, University of Toronto, 1975, chapter 2.

10. For discussion of these points see Cynthia Enloe, *Ethnic Conflict and Political Development,* Boston: Little Brown, 1973; Connor, *op. cit.;* Rawkins, *op. cit.,* chapter 18.

11. For detailed development of this point, see Rawkins, "Outsiders as Insiders: The Implications of Minority Nationalism in Scotland and Wales," *Comparative Politics,* Vol. 10, 4, July 78: 519-534.

12. Richard J. Barnet and Ronald E. Müller, *Global Reach: The Power of the Multinational Corporations,* New York: Simon and Schuster, 1974: 302.

13. For a detailed argument on these lines, see Poulantzas, *op. cit.,* and Stephen Hymer, "The Multinational Corporation: Your Home is our Home," *Canadian Dimension,* Vol. 8, 6, March-April 1972: 29-35, 47-49.

14. Hymer, "The Multinational Corporation and Uneven Development," *op. cit.,* 128-9.

15. Michael Barratt-Brown, *From Labourism to Socialism,* Nottingham, Bertrand Russell Peace Foundation, 1972.

16. Holland, *op. cit.,* 329-330; Dennis Swann, *The Economics of the Common Market,* Harmondsworth: Penguin Books, Third Edition, 1975: 167-70; Anthony Sampson, *The New Europeans,* London: Panther Books, 1971: 134-5; David Blake and Robert S. Walters, *The Politics of Global Economic Relations,* Englewood Cliffs, New Jersey: Prentice-Hall, 1976: 108.

17. See Poulantzas, *op. cit.,* both Hymer citations, Robin Murray, "Capital and the Nation-State," *New Left Review,* 67, May-June 1971: 84-109.

18. Kari Levitt, "Towards Decolonization: Canada and Quebec," *Canadian Forum,* Vol. 51, 614, March 1972: 2-3.

19. Gellner, *op. cit.,* 155.

20. *Ibid.,* 155-7.

21. See Nairn, *op. cit.,* 22.

22. For examples, see Patricia Elton Mayo, *op. cit.;* Rawkins, "Rich Welsh or Poor British? A Sociological Analysis of Political Mobilization and Modes of Activism in the Welsh Nationalist Movement," Paper presented at the *Annual Meetings of the American Political Science Association,* Chicago, 1974; James Jacob, "The Basques of France: A Case of Peripheral Ethnonationalism in Europe," *Political Anthropology,* Vol. 1, 1, March 1975: 67-87.

23. Gellner, *op. cit.,* 162; similar points are made by Enloe, *op. cit.,* 28, and Connor, *op. cit.,* 341-2.

24. See Jurgen Habermas, "Technology and Science as 'Ideology'," in *Toward A Rational Society,* London: Heinemann, 1971: 92.

25. Barnet and Müller, *op. cit.,* 26-44.

26. Quoted in *ibid.,* 54.

27. See Habermas, *op. cit.,* 91-112; see also, Claus Mueller, *The Politics of Communication,* New York: Oxford University Press, 1973: 109-111.

28. See Habermas, *op. cit.,* 112-115.

29. On distorted communication, see Mueller, *op. cit.,* 13-42, 86-111.

30. See Max Weber, "Bureaucracy," Gerth and Mills, *op. cit.,* 196-244; also Anthony Giddens, *Capitalism and Modern Social Theory,* London: Cambridge University Press, 1971: 169-184, 232-6.

31. Giddens, *op. cit.,* 184.

32. *Ibid.,* 118-119.

33. Abraham Maslow, *Toward a Psychology of Being,* Princeton, N.J.: Van Nostrand, 1962.

34. This paper represents a series of further, more general reflections on a more directly empirically-based argument presented elsewhere; see Rawkins, "Outsiders as Insiders," *op. cit.;* also, "Welsh Nationalism and the Crisis of the British State," presented at *Glendon Conference on Minority Nationalism,* Glendon College, York University, Toronto, March, 1977; "Rich Welsh or Poor British," *op. cit.*

CONCLUSION

Ronald M. Grant and E. Spencer Wellhofer

These papers form a patchwork quilt in their convergence on one major theme: the impact of economic change on inequality. In the collection, a model of the role of organization and political structure is suggested in economic and ethnic issues. According to Rawkins, who draws heavily from Weber, MNCs emerge as economic change agents promoting the rational scientific technology of the center.[1] On the periphery, and at the mercy of the forces of economic change emanating from the center, are minority ethnic groups sharing marginal economic status. Minority ethnic groups undergo increased awareness of their common identity for two possible reasons: "functionalist" and "reactive" explanations of ethnic identification.[2] In the functionalist argument, ethnic nationalism serves a psychocultural need for a community facing the anonymous forces of change. In the reactive theory, ethnic identification and conflict are responses to the economic forces *and* policies by dominant groups of the center. For Rawkins, the emerging dominant group is the MNC, or the MNC in alliance with the national government. Rawkins intertwines ethno-nationalism and ethnic change, concluding with an argument that favors the functionalist school.

The practices of the MNC and other multi-nationalist economic organizations generate increased awareness of sub-national ethnic groups in their disadvantaged position and discriminated status. Enloe presents the organizational response of ethnic groups to the MNC. Fontaine and Hill, in their case study of the Caribbean, go further; they delineate the political dimension of the reactive theory. They provide the only clear-cut instance in the four papers of an important intervening variable essential in the analysis: the state no longer is a partner with the MNC. This important observation influences the more complex model proposed later.

The MNC serves as the vehicle for expanding the rational scientific culture of the metropolitan center and through cooperation with groups in the host society reinforces the existing status quo. This creates greater economic inequalities in the society. The resulting socio-economic change may bring class cleavages to the foreground, as it has in Brazil. If the host society contains multiple ethnic groups, the economic inequalities of these groups will play a crucial role in the emergence of ethno-nationalism, the argument put forth by Enloe. If the *economic* division of labor corresponds with the *cultural* division of labor, some ethnic groups develop a collective and cumulative social and economic disadvantage.[3] In such circumstances class cleavages become isomorphic with ethnic cleavages.

Ethno-nationalism may develop at some distance from the political-economic center, and the conditions under which it emerges may vary. The schematic diagram of economic change and socio-political reaction in Figure 1 indicates the dynamics of change. Although the MNC is a general symbol for economic forces of change imposed from the outside, it is only one expression of a larger development, the globalization of the economy.[4] In the diagram, arrows imply association; the generality of the model and the tentative understanding of linkages prohibits claiming causal relationships.

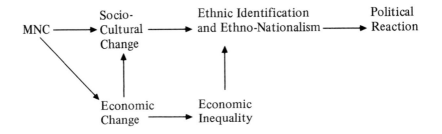

Figure 1.

Three different conceptions of the multi-national corporation are helpful in understanding the role of the MNC. Each view offers an interpretation of the relationship among MNCs, the host society, and indigenous ethnic groups. Robert Gilpin identifies a Liberal, a Marxist, and a Mercantilist perspective of the multi-national.[5] The liberal conception sees ''the trans-national actor in general and the multi-national corporation in particular. . . undermining the nation-state'' due to their superior performance in an emerging interdependent world economy,[6] because the MNCs command the most advanced development, production, and marketing technologies. They embody the rational scientific culture of the center and function as change agents. This conception is not necessarily contradictory to the Marxist conceptions of the MNC as ''merely the expression of capitalist exploitation and imperialism,'' where the MNC becomes the primary causal agent for continual economic inequality and accompanying exploitation.[7] Gilpin's position that multi- and trans-national economic organizations are also political units requires some refinement, but it is not contradictory to the above argument and general model. The Mercantilist interpretation places emphasis on the political role served by the MNC. In brief, this position argues that MNCs are merely the representatives of dominant political orders. The Mercantilist position focuses on parallels between colonial trading companies and contemporary MNCs: the essential similarity lies in the fact that both serve political and economic interests of a mother country. Some nations do not always stand behind home based MNCs. Moreover, even economically developed states circumscribe the MNCs, as the recent example of Canada and the provincial government of Quebec illustrates.[8]

We are not rejecting the Mercantilist position entirely. All nation-states, especially capitalist ones, are stratified. The MNC serves some strata more than others. And, if political organization can counter economic arrangement, a more complex model is needed.

The complex model must take into account an organizational approach integrated with factors influencing economic change and producing sociopolitical reaction. Legitimacy and organizational resources are important at three levels of political organization: sub-national, national, and international.

The MNC represents an external change agent in a host society. Since permission of the state is required, the MNC usually enters into an alliance with the host society government.[9] Cooperation of the MNC with the host society's elite initially reinforces the existing stratification system. Stratification systems are not simply class-based but may incorporate socio-cultural, geographical, religious, racial, ethnic, or other factors in marking community diversity. The MNCs' control of advanced technology and efficient organization gives easy entry to domestic economies. The MNC alliance with host groups usually results in mutual cooperation—often, however, to the unequal advantage of the participants.

Consequences for the host society follow. The resulting socio-economic change brings class cleavage to the foreground. By generating or reinforcing inequities, and contrasting affluence and advanced technology with poverty and tradition, the MNC heightens relative and real deprivation. Second, the MNC represents forces of economic change beyond the control of any group in society. Hence, other sources of legitimacy—Geertz's primordial sentiments—must be rallied to counter overwhelming odds of economic rationalization.

For any social class, ethnic awareness often emerges under conditions of economic change. Ethno-nationalism more readily develops among the economically disadvantaged rather than among the economically dominant groups. The self-interest of the group in alliance with the MNC dominates. Ethnic groups benefiting from their relationship to a MNC will not stress differences with their benefactor. On the other hand, ethno-nationalism does not always develop among the disadvantaged, and when it does it is not always effective. Accordingly, we must specify conditions for its appearance and effectiveness.

Fontaine highlights the role of political organization for mobilizing groups into an ethnic-nationalism force. But the political economy of organization varies among groups, and numerous conditions influence organizational development. Fontaine's analysis suggests two factors: leadership and communication to transform political resources (such as the vote) into formidable political weapons. Rawkins suggests another: "the moralization of hurts." [10] The mobilization of ethnic consciousness requires leadership and a moral interpretation of the "senseless suffering" so that the consequences of the current order are viewed as unjust in the eyes of the disadvantaged. Each of these elements must be present for an ethical and moral interpretation of suffering to portray the current order as inappropriate and unjust. A counter elite can create a counter ideology from the "moralization of hurts." For example, the diffusion of the ideas of equality and justice embodied in the French and Russian Revolutions made it impossibly difficult to sustain the moral systems supporting the monarchical regimes. [11] The newly emerging classes provided the leadership and facilitated the organizational response.

Several authors suggest conditions enhancing the emergence of ethnic consciousness. Fontaine presents the development of leadership to mobilize ethnic sensitivities for political purposes. Organizational skills, communication channels, and the "moralization of hurts" produce a political movement capable of winning control of the state and modifying the relationship of the MNC to the host society.

The last point suggests the importance of viewing the relationship between the MNC and ethnic-nationalism in organizational terms, particularly political organization. Organization softens uncontrolled and debilitating economic change; the most effective counter organization is the state. Ethnic and class organizations may be effective in gaining control over the state, but without that control they will be ineffective in mitigating the challenge of multi-national economic organizations. Due to the technical, economic, and political resources of the MNC, control of the state is essential if the MNC is to be contained and made useful for economic development.

The modern nation-state needs to be understood, in the context of an international order and the evolution of political organization, as the most efficient and effective instrument for collective goal achievement. These four papers stress the need for greater attention to the role of organization in explaining relationships between economic change and socio-political reaction. As Marx, Weber, and others have made clear, ethical explanations are readily available for both economic progress and change, but in order to understand historical developments, it may be fruitful to focus upon political organization and how it fits into the equation.

FOOTNOTES

1. It is not simply material self-interest and gain which attracts certain types of elites to the MNC. Particularly in poor countries, bureaucrats and the military are culturally closest to the scientific-technological culture emanating from the international "center" and borne by the MNC. Extending this hypothesis, Eric Nordlinger suggested that military governments are especially ineffectual in dealing with communal and ethnic problems. They simply possess an organizational and value orientation emphasizing rationality and universality in contrast to the norms and values of affective attachment which underlie ethnic identification.

2. Hechter, Michael, *Internal Colonialism*. See reference in Introduction.

3. Hechter, Michael, *Internal Colonialism*, 38.

4. It is commonplace today to speak of economic interdependence. This, however, emphasizes relationships between economics and not the real or perceived effects on individuals. Concerned with behavior in terms of socio-political reaction to economic change and inequality, we are trying to take the view of individual actors, not of complex systems.

5. Robert Gilpin, "The Political Economy of the Multinational Corporation: Three Contrasting Perspectives," *American Political Science Review*, LXX, No 1, March 1976: 184-91.

6. *Ibid.*, 186.

7. *Ibid.*, 187.

8. *Ibid.*, 188-89.

9. James Reston, "Quebec: Challenge for U.S.," *New York Times*. Also see, "J-M Chief Says Impact of Quebec Talk Unearned," *Denver Post*, 27 January 1977: 47.

10. *From Max Weber: Essays in Sociology.* H.H. Gerth and C. Wright Mills, trans. and eds., Oxford University Press: New York 1969: 281.

11. Rheinhart Bendix, *Nation-Building and Citizenship*, New York: Anchor Books, 1969: 212-55.

MONOGRAPH SERIES IN WORLD AFFAIRS

The Social Science Foundation and
Graduate School of International Studies
University of Denver

ACTING EDITOR (1977-1978) . . . . Edward A. Hawley
EDITOR (1978) . . . . Karen Ann Feste
MANAGING EDITOR . . . . Dorothea W. Blair
ASSISTANT EDITOR . . . . Mary Jane Lewis

The monographs in this series are published four times a year. All correspondence should be addressed to:

MONOGRAPH SERIES IN WORLD AFFAIRS
University of Denver

Graduate School of International Studies
Denver, Colorado 80208

W.A.E. Skurnik, Editor, René Lamarchand, Kenneth W. Grundy and Charles F. Andrain. *African Political Thought: Lumumba, Nkrumah, and Touré.*

Volume 6, 1968-1969 Series

Frederick H. Gareau. *The Cold War 1947-1967: A Quantitative Study.*

Henderson B. Braddick. *Germany, Czechoslovakia, and the "Grand Alliance" in the May Crisis, 1938.*

Robert L. Freidheim. *Understanding the Debate on Ocean Resources.*

Richard L. Siegel. *Evaluating the Results of Foreign Policy: Soviet and American Efforts in India.*

Volume 7, 1969-1970 Series

Quincy Wright. *On Predicting International Relations, The Year 2000.*

James N. Rosenau. *Race in International Politics: A Dialogue in Five Parts.*

William S. Tuohy and Barry Ames. *Mexican University Students in Politics: Rebels without Allies?*

Karl H. Hoerning. *Secondary Modernization: Societal Changes of Newly Developing Nations—A Theoretical Essay in Comparative Sociology.*

Volume 8, 1970-1971 Series

Young W. Kihl. *Conflict Issues and International Civil Aviation: Three Cases.*

Morton Schwartz. *The "Motive Forces" of Soviet Foreign Policy, A Reappraisal.*

Joseph I. Coffey. *Deterrence in the 1970s.*

Edward Miles. *International Administration of Space Exploration and Exploitation.*

Volume 9, 1971-1972 Series

Edwin G. Corr. *The Political Process in Colombia.*

Shelton L. Williams. *Nuclear Nonproliferation in International Politics: The Japanese Case.*

Sue Ellen M. Charlton. *The French Left and European Integration.*

Volume 10, 1972-1973 Series

Robert W. Dean. *Nationalism and Political Change in Eastern Europe: The Slovak Question and the Czechoslovak Reform Movement.*

M. Donald Hancock. *The Bundeswehr and the National People's Army: A Comparative Study of German Civil-Military Polity.*

Louis René Beres. *The Management of World Power: A Theoretical Analysis.*

George A. Kourvetaris and Betty A. Dobratz. *Social Origins and Political Orientations of Officer Corps in a World Perspective.*

Volume 11, 1973-1974 Series

Waltraud Q. Morales. *Social Revolution: Theory and Historical Application.*

David O'Shea. *Education, the Social System, and Development.*

Robert H. Bates. *Patterns of Uneven Development: Causes and Consequences in Zambia.*

Robert L. Peterson. *Career Motivations of Administrators and Their Impact in the European Community.*

Volume 12, 1974-1975 Series

Craig Liske and Barry Rundquist. *The Politics of Weapons Procurement: The Role of Congress.*

Barry M. Schutz and Douglas Scott. *Natives and Settlers: A Comparative Analysis of the Politics of Opposition and Mobilization in Northern Ireland and Rhodesia.*

Vincent B. Khapoya. *The Politics of Decision: A Comparative Study of African Policy Toward the Liberation Movements.*

Louis René Beres. *Transforming World Politics: The National Roots of World Peace.*

Volume 13, 1975-1976 Series

Wayne S. Vucinich. *A Study in Social Survival: Katun in the Bileća Rudine.*

Jan F. Triska and Paul M. Johnson. *Political Development and Political Change in Eastern Europe: A Comparative Study.*

Louis L. Ortmayer. *Conflict, Compromise, and Conciliation: West German-Polish Normalization 1966-1976.*

James B. Bruce. *Politics of Soviet Policy Formation: Khrushchev's Innovative Policies in Education and Agriculture.*

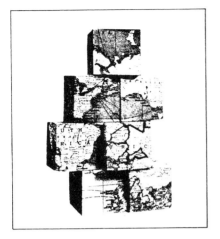

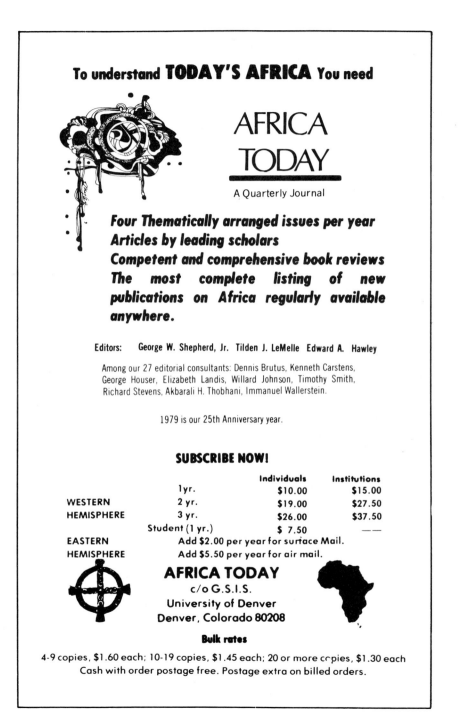